Creating Celebration

CAKES
AND SUGAR FLOWERS

Enjoy the magic of creating your own celebration cakes with the help and guidance from our team of expert cake decorators.

A collection of thirty two wonderful projects for all occasions, complete with simple step-by-step pictures and full instructions.

Our highly talented decorators share their inspirational skills, ideas and professional knowledge to help you decorate your cake with Sugarpaste, Marzipan, Royal Icing, Buttercream, Flowerpaste and Modelling Paste.

First published in 2006 by PME Arts & Crafts, a division of Knightsbridge PME Ltd
Reprinted 2009

© Knightsbridge PME Ltd

ISBN 0-9552763-0-6
978-09552763-0-9

Acknowledgements

Precision Machining Engineers (Harrow) Limited was established in 1956 and became a limited company in 1958. The company was founded by Malcolm Craig, a resident of Harrow and initially provided a range of engineering services to local business.

As the company grew, it concentrated on tool making and plastic injection moulding in particular and as a consequence, was able to supply products and components for such things as medical and musical instruments, gardening equipment and the motor trade.

PME earned a reputation for producing high quality, which lead to the gaining of lucrative contracts from the defence industry.

In the early 1970's PME first became involved in cake decorating and were asked by the Army Catering Corps in Hampshire to produce 2,000 stainless steel royal icing rulers. Other product ideas soon followed leading to the formation of PME Sugarcraft Ltd.

In addition to products for use with royal icing, PME began to manufacture items for use with sugarpaste and marzipan.

One of the most popular items ever to be introduced was the miniature flower blossom plunger cutters, which are still available today and can be found in the kit boxes of most cake decorators.

Other products which have earned PME the reputation as the leading manufacturer of quality cake decorating equipment are their very recognisable yellow handled modelling tools, seamless stainless steel icing tubes and crimpers, textured rolling pins, tilting turntable and plunger cutter ranges.

PME exhibits at international trade shows and continues to develop new products, which are distributed worldwide. This book is another first for the company and brings together the work of well known UK cake decorators who have been associated with PME over the years and now share their ideas and creations using PME products.

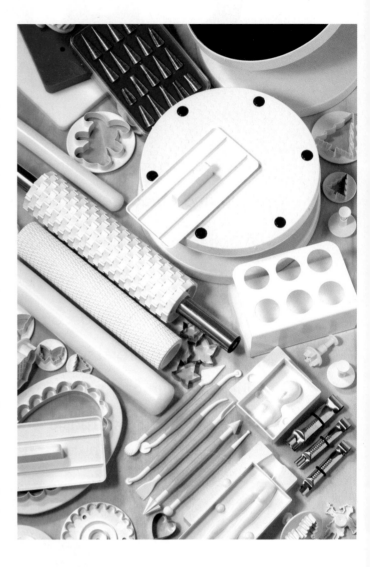

PME products are available worldwide and for further information contact
Knightsbridge PME Ltd, Chadwell Heath Lane, Romford, Essex, RM6 4NP, England
Tel: +44 (0) 20 8590 5959   Fax: +44 (0) 20 8590 7373
website: www.cakedecoration.co.uk

Commissioning Director   David Gray
Knightsbridge PME Ltd

Creative Editor   Pat Trunkfield
Knightsbridge PME Ltd

Editor   Sheila Lampkin
Lampkin Media Services

Design   Jacqueline South
Jax Design

Photography   Bob Challinor
Ghost Images

Printed by Fuller Davies Ltd

Contents

Sugarpaste

Sugarpaste is a wonderful icing, ideal for all cake decorators including beginners, enthusiasts and professional confectioners, its ease of handling and versatility ensuring fun and creativity.

A soft eating roll out icing, Sugarpaste is also known as Fondant Icing, Gelatine Icing and Plastic Icing. Although often considered to be a modern day icing, sugarpaste in a variety of forms has been used as a decorative material for many centuries.

A wide range of manufactured sugarpastes are easily available in many countries and these products will provide continuity of consistency, flavour and colour; the basic recipes below may be useful if you wish to prepare your own icing.

Simple Sugarpaste

icing sugar - sifted 500g(1lb)
liquid glucose 30ml(2 tablespoons)
white vegetable fat 25g(1oz)
egg white 25 - 50g(1 - 2oz)

1 Place the icing sugar, glucose and white fat into a bowl and begin mixing together.

2 Add the egg white a little at a time, enough to bind the ingredients.

3 Turn the paste out onto a work surface and gently knead until smooth and silky. Use icing sugar for dusting if necessary.

4 Store in an air tight plastic bag.

PME Pointers

Secure sugarpaste to a sponge cake with jam or buttercream and for a fruit cake, pre-coated with marzipan, use clear alcohol or cooled boiled water.

Coloured Sugarpaste

The versatility of sugarpaste, naturally encourages the use of colour.

1 Food colourings are available in various forms e.g. liquid, paste, jel and powder. To add colour to sugarpaste aim to choose a concentrated paste or jel colour, this reduces the quantity of colour required and allows the icing to be coloured without becoming sticky. The easiest way to add these colours is with a cocktail stick or toothpick.

2 To colour large quantities of sugarpaste, colour a small piece of paste first in a deeper shade than required and then knead this into the bulk of the paste.

3 Wonderful marbled effects can be achieved by only partially kneading the colour or coloured pastes together.

PME Pointers

To coat with dark coloured sugarpaste keep the icing sugar for dusting to a minimum this reduces the possibility of white sugar marks on the cake.

To coat a round cake

1 Prepare the paste by kneading well then shape into a smooth ball.

2 Place onto the work surface and with a light dusting of icing sugar begin to roll out the paste.

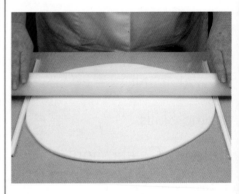

3 To ensure an even thickness marzipan/sugarpaste spacers may be placed either side of the paste to roll it out.

4 Roll out sufficient paste to cover the top and sides of the cake, plus a little extra, as it is always easier to coat a cake if the paste is larger than the actual cake.

Ideally the rolling pin should be long enough to stretch over the whole of the paste.

5 Polish the paste with a smoother using a circular motion, this will remove any blemishes, marks and excess dusting sugar.

6 Place the rolling pin in the centre of the paste, carefully wrap the paste over the pin and lift up onto the cake, positioning as central as possible.

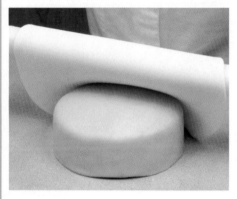

7 Lay the paste gently over the top and sides of the cake easing any folds or gathers into the excess paste at the bottom.

PME Pointers

Remove any air bubbles by piercing with a scriber, needle or pin.

PME Pointers

For difficult shaped cakes e.g. numbers, it may be easier to coat the top and sides separately and use crimpers to bring the two cut edges together or pipe a decorative border

8 Ease the paste onto the sides of the cake using a slightly cupped hand and an upwards movement.

9 Trim the paste to the base of the cake with a palette knife.

10 To obtain the best finish, use two smoothers one to polish the sides of the cake and the

second to hold the cake, firmly in position. Complete the cake covering, by polishing the top edges, taking the smoother from the sides up onto the top surface.

Coating cakes with corners e.g. square, hexagonal & novelty cakes

1 Always try to roll the sugarpaste out the basic shape of the cake.

2 Once the paste is over the cake, concentrate on the corners.

3 Ease the excess paste out at the base of the corner, before using a cupped hand to bring the paste gently into position.

4 Finish all of the corners before securing any flat surfaces. Trim the paste.

5 Use two smoothers to bring the paste into a sharper corner shape.

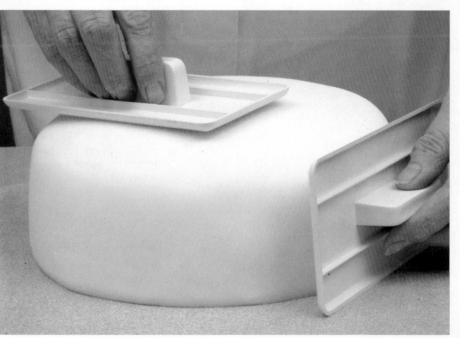

Loveable Teddies

*Teddy bears are a timeless favourite and very popular as a decoration for cakes.
These, easy to use, cutters will help you achieve a great effect in record time.*

by Nadene Hurst

1 Marzipan the cake and cover with baby blue sugarpaste, including the board. Leave for twenty four hours for the paste to dry.

2 Colour approximately 30g (1oz) of flowerpaste in a deeper blue than the cake covering. Roll out thinly, place the template on top and cut round using the cutting wheel. For the smaller curves use a craft knife. Place on run-out film and leave to dry.

3 Mix together 60g(2oz) each of white sugarpaste and flowerpaste. Colour for the teddy bears. To make the colour use a mixture of orange, egg yellow and brown until you reach a shade you like.

4 Roll out the paste to 2.5mm (1/8in) thickness and cut out a large teddy bear. Separate the head and body with a curved line. Then cut off the arm with a curve as shown.

5 Use the largest Briar Rose cutter to indent a line round the body, mark a circle on each of the three remaining paws with the smallest cutter, and a circle on each ear using a No.18 icing tip. Add tiny stitches down the body, arms and legs. Dry flat, but place the single arm against the cut out number to dry in the correct position.

6 Take a ball of paste, dust with cornflour, then press into the large ball mould and turn out to make the head. Indent tiny stitches down the face. Attach to the flat head which was cut away from the body, with the ears showing.

PME Pointers — To obtain the correct size of paste for the mould, roll a rough ball and try it in the mould first. Then adjust the amount accordingly.

7 Roll out a thin piece of paste, cut out a medium sized circle, then move the cutter across to make an elipse shape. Attach to the front of the head and make a hole for the nose and two for the eyes. Fill these with small balls of black paste. Airbrush a shadow round the base of the head and the circle of the body. Leave to dry.

8 Cut out a narrow strip of blue sugarpaste and stick it on the top half at the back of the number one, to lift it level with the depth of the teddy. Place it in position and slide the teddy underneath at an angle as shown. Secure both with edible glue. Position the head, support it underneath with a small circle of paste to keep it level.

9 Trace the lettering and pipe it onto the cake in the darker blue colour, using a No.2 icing tip.

10 To make the small teddies, roll out the paste to 1.5mm ($1/16$in) thick, cut out six with the medium size cutter. Indent stitches down the bodies and legs, then mark a defining line round the bodies in the same way as the larger one. Use a No.18 tip to indent the paws, and a No.16 on the ears.

11 For the heads use the smallest ball mould. To increase the size to fit the body, roll out some paste 2.5mm($1/8$in) thick, and cut out medium sized circles. Stick them over the half balls and gather round the base, making them bigger. Place on the cut out teddies and proceed in the same way as the larger one.

12 Airbrush shadows round the sides of the heads and round the edges of the bodies, this will give them a three dimentional appearance. Cut out three small blue circles of flowerpaste, divide into quarters and attach them under the chin of the small teddies.

PME Pointers

As an alternative to airbrushing use dry dusting powder to create the shadows.

13 With the scriber mark 2.5cm(1in) away from each corner at the base of the cake. Cut the two side templates out of thin card. Place the outside one on the cake with the tip over a corner point, and the flat edge at the base,

with the inside edge at the marked position. Scribe a line along the outside edge with a scriber needle. Reverse the template and repeat the process on the opposite side of the corner.

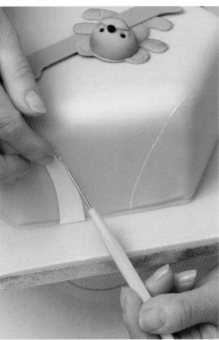

PME Pointers

To allow for the variation in depth of different cakes, do not scribe the line beyond the top edge of the cake.

14 Roll out white flowerpaste thinly for the ribbon tails. Place the template on top and run a line of stitches round, very close to the edge. Remove the template and cut round using a cutting wheel, close to the stitches. Place on kitchen roll and dust with a pearlised dusting powder.

15 Attach to the side of the cake with edible glue, use the scribed line as a guide for the position. Trim off on the top point of the cake. Continue round the cake, reversing the template for the opposite sides.

16 Cut out twelve more ribbon tails using the inside pattern, attach these inside the first set, leaving equal gaps between them. Trim at the top where all four points meet.

17 For the bows cut twelve strips with stitches down the edges, 2.5cm(1in) wide and 7.5cm(3in) long. Fold over and gather the ends together. Slide on to a piece of 1cm ($\frac{1}{2}$in) dowelling to dry. Place two together at a slight angle and cover the centre with a narrow strip of paste. Attach one to each corner.

18 Make a very long, narrow roll of paste and place it round the base of the cake. Start the roll using your fingertips, then continue with a side scraper, rolling it from side to side across the top. This creates a smooth, even roll.

19 Attach the teddies to the side of the cake and cover the edge of the board with matching ribbon.

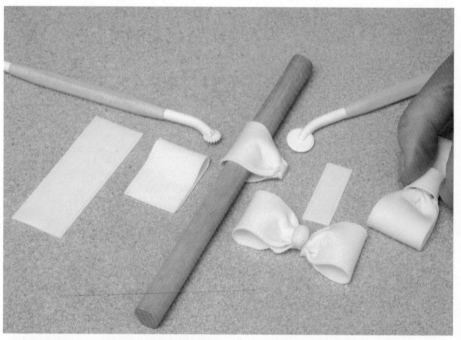

Dancing Clowns

Many hours of fun have been spent just watching those clowns spinning round and round. As the spinning top goes faster, their brightly coloured clothes merge to just a flash of colour.

by Karen Goble

1 Roll out the grey sugarpaste, dampen the board with a little boiled water, cover the board and trim the edges. Texture the surface with a ribbed rolling pin. Roll over the board in one complete movement. Turn the board a quarter turn, then texture again, this will make a fine squared pattern.

2 With a veining tool and a straight edge mark in some lines to give a tiled effect. Leave to dry.

3 Bake two madeira cakes in large mixing bowls. Allow the cakes to cool in the bowl then turn out onto the work surface. Trim the large surface of each cake flat and cut the rounded sides of the cakes to a cone shape.

5 For the top of the spinning top roll out 150g(5¼oz) yellow sugarpaste to about 2.5cm (1in) thick, cut out a 9cm (3½in) circle. Then roll out 85g(3½oz) of red sugar paste to the same thickness cut out a 5cm(2in) circle. Smooth the edges of the circles to form a soft bevel, then place both circles centrally on top of the cake, secure with a little water.

6 Colour small amounts of white sugarpaste with eight different colours plus a flesh colour for the face and hands, roll out each colour then using the clown cutter cut out eight clowns, place onto a flat surface.

4 With the large flat surface of the cake at the base, coat each cake with a thin layer of buttercream. Cover one cake with rolled red sugarpaste and the other with rolled green sugarpaste. Turn the cakes over and apply a thin coat of jam to one surface. Join the cakes together then place the 'spinning top' centrally onto the cake board.

It is a good idea to chill the cake prior to carving out the shape.

7 With a cutting wheel remove the hands and feet. Set aside the feet for later. Continue removing the head, hats and hair, discard the faces and hands.

8 Roll out flesh coloured paste and cut out eight faces and eight pairs of hands.

9 Reform the clowns mixing up the colours. Place around the top of the cake securing with a little water.

10 Roll out some yellow and purple sugarpaste and use a 20mm briar rose cutter to cut out enough circles to go all the way around the centre join of the spinning top. Roll out a little orange paste and cut out enough small squares to go in the centres of the purple circles, secure around the cake with a little water.

11 Push a 30cm(12in) dowel down through the centre top of the cake through both layers of the cake to the base board, mark the dowel at the top of the cake.

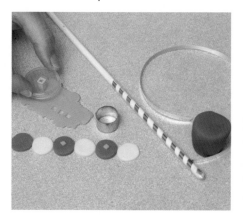

12 Remove the dowel, then twist a small amount of parcel ribbon around the top of the dowel starting from the mark on the dowel. Secure with a little double sided tape. Shape a handle with 25g(³/₄oz) of purple sugarpaste, push onto the top of the dowel and place back into the cake.

13 Place a heaped teaspoon of bright red coloured royal icing into a piping bag fitted with a 1.5 tube. Pipe three small buttons down the centre of each clowns costume. Also pipe a red nose on each face.

14 Paint a smile on each clown using red food colour and a fine paintbrush; for the eyes paint two small black crosses. Finish the board with a ribbon and double sided tape.

PME Pointers

For a special finish always trim the baseboard with a ribbon to complement the cake. The best way to secure the ribbon in place is to use double-sided tape.

Easter Time

Celebrate springtime when young animals and birds are born and bright fresh flowers grow in our gardens.

by Karen Goble

1 1 Place the round cake onto the large round board and with a sharp knife hollow a circle about 10cm(4in) round and 2.5cm(1in) deep in the middle of the cake. Split the cake and add jam if required. Coat the cake with buttercream and cover with rolled green sugarpaste. Smooth the top and sides with a cake smoother.

Checklist • Checklist • Checklist

- Madeira cake 1 round 26cm(10in)
- Madeira cake 2 half egg shapes baked in an egg pan
- Round cake board 38cm (15in)
- Buttercream
- Jam (optional)
- Sugarpaste - green 1.25kg (2½lb)
- Sugarpaste - lemon 1kg (2lb)
- Royal icing 500g (1lb)
- Flowerpaste 100g (1lb)
- Food colours - green, brown, black, orange, pink and yellow
- Large rolling pin
- Sharp knife
- Cake smoother
- Piping tubes 1.5, 51, 52,
- Duck cutter set
- Rabbit cutter set
- Butterfly small
- Primrose cutter set
- Plunger blossom set
- Non-stick board and pin
- Ball tool
- Star tool
- Stiff card
- Paint brush and pallet
- Board ribbon
- Double sided tape

PME Pointers

Do not use too much jam to stick the halves together as it may squeeze out of the sides.

2 Colour four tablespoons of royal icing with green food colour, place into a piping bag fitted with a No.51 tube then randomly pipe some reeds around the base of the cake making some longer than others.

3 Cover each side of the egg with buttercream then roll out 500g (1lb) of lemon sugarpaste for each side of the egg, cover each cake then smooth with smoother. Place one side of the cake back into a clean half egg shape pan. Spread jam over the middle and place the other side on top. Rotate the cake in the tin and smooth the join.

paste and press the cone down onto the board. With a small rolling pin thin the outer edges this will make a mexican hat shape. Use this technique and the primrose cutters to cut out a selection of flowers in different colours and sizes.

PME Pointers

Brush the cutting edges of metal cutters frequently with a stiff bristle brush to remove any flower paste remnants.

4 **Ducks** - Roll out a small amount of flowerpaste and cut out six large ducks, eleven smaller ducklings and a family of white rabbits.

5 Paint all the duck beaks yellow. Paint two of the large duck heads with green and their bodies with light brown; paint the chest and wings slightly darker brown. Paint two large ducks and seven small ducklings with light brown then darken the wings. Paint the wings and eyes of the remaining ducks and ducklings with a little black leaving the bodies white. Allow to dry and then paint the other side in a similar manner.

6 **Rabbits** - Colour a little paste grey and some brown, roll and cut out three families of rabbits, paint all the rabbit faces with black food colour. On each one add two dots for eyes and one dot for a nose. Add a small painted 'w' for the mouth. Leave to dry.

7 Retain a tablespoon of white royal icing in a small bowl. Colour the rest of the icing with blue. Cover the rim of the board with this icing using a pallet knife. Make sure the icing is quite thick and that it goes right up to the side of the cake. Arrange the ducks around the cake grouping together in three families.

8 Colour small amounts of flowerpaste with yellow, pink, orange. Make a small cone of

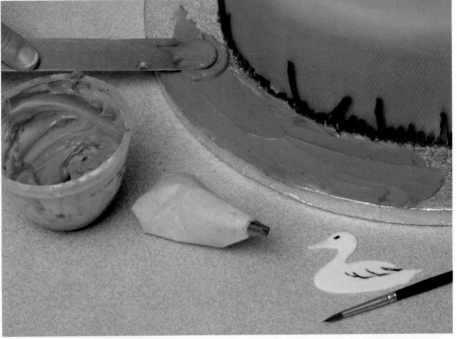

9 Press the small end of the ball tool into the outer edge of the primrose petals then with a five star tool push down into the centre of each flower, this gives an ideal centre for the primrose or if coloured a primula. Leave to dry.

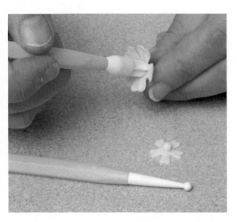

10 With flower paste of different colours, roll and cut out a selection of blossoms using all the different sizes. Place the blossom onto some sponge foam then press the plunger down. This will cup the blossom and eject the blossom from the cutter.

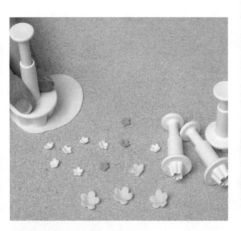

card to dry this allows the wings to hold their shape.

11 Fold a piece of card into an 'M' shape. Roll out a small amount of white flowerpaste and cut out two small butterflies. Place into the

12 When the butterflies are dry paint the ends of the wings with yellow and the body light brown. Assemble the butterflies and flowers onto the egg and place few blossoms and the families of rabbits on the round cake, secure with royal icing. Pipe green royal icing leaves in between the flowers with tube No.51 and No.52.

13 Fix a ribbon around the board, secure with double sided tape.

Santa's Sleigh Ride

Here comes Santa Claus setting off in his sleigh to deliver presents around the world. His team include Dasher, Dancer, Prancer, Vixen, Comet, Cupid, Donner, Blitzen and last but not least Rudolph, the red nosed reindeer.

by Karen Goble

1 Moisten the cake board and cover with 750g(1½lb) of rolled sugarpaste. Refer to the diagram to cut the cake. Stand each cake up right on a thin oblong board.

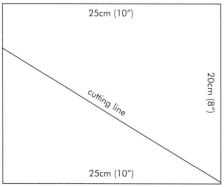

This is the bottom of the cake

25cm (10")

20cm (8")

cutting line

25cm (10")

This is the bottom of the cake

Checklist • Checklist • Checklist

- Fruit Cake 26x20cm (10x8in) oblong
- Apricot glaze (jelly)
- Marzipan 1.750g (3½lbs)
- Clear alcohol (boiled water)
- Sugarpaste 2500g (5lb) white
- Flowerpaste 100g (3½oz) green
- Flowerpaste 100g(3½oz) white
- Royal Icing 500g (1lb) white
- Glitter flakes - clear
- Food colours green, red, black, brown, blue, gold
- Rolling pin
- Cake smoother
- Non-stick board
- Christmas tree cutter set
- Cutting wheel
- Reindeer cutters
- Paintbrush & pallet
- Father Christmas cutter small
- 1.5 piping tube & bag
- Creative plaque embossing cutters small & large
- Pallet knife
- Drum board 36x26cm (14x10in)
- Two thin boards 26x8cm (10x3in) oblong
- Board ribbon
- Double sided tape

2 Coat the cakes with apricot glaze and cover with rolled marzipan. Dampen the marzipan with clear alcohol or boiled water then cover with sugarpaste. Stand the cakes onto the board placing the larger cake at the back.

3 Roll out some green flowerpaste and cut out a selection of Christmas trees.

4 Cut down the centre of some trees with a cutting wheel. place to dry on a flat board dusted with cornflour.

5 Colour a small amount of royal icing with green. Use one complete tree and three half trees. Pipe a line of royal icing down the centre of the complete tree then place the two half trees down the middle, support with a little foam. Pipe another line of icing and place the remaining half tree between the other two, support and leave to dry.

6 Make a total of four large, four medium and two small three dimentional trees.

belt and boots in black and his face with a little pink, add a dot in the eyes with black.

10 Pipe the beard and trims of his clothes with white royal icing, leave to dry. When dry turn the paste over and paint the other side.

11 Roll out white flowerpaste to 3mm (¹/₈in) thick. Use the large and small creative plaque cutters fitted with the raised embosser to cut out one of each size, press the button to emboss the pattern. With a

cutting wheel cut down the centre length ways. Stand up onto the cut edge and curve the ends round so the pointed ends just touch each other.

7 Colour a small amount of white flowerpaste with a little brown (not too dark). Roll and cut out eight large reindeer and one smaller reindeer. Paint the back and the antlers of the reindeer with a little brown food colour also paint the noses with black except the nose of the smallest reindeer - paint this red, this is Rudolf. Leave to dry.

8 When the pieces are completely dry, add some small dots of white to the backs of the reindeer.

9 Cut out Father Christmas from white paste, press down the plunger to emboss the features and outline the clothes. Use food colours to paint his suit red, his

12 Roll out a base for the sledge, place the top pieces onto the base and cut around the edge

The colour needs to be concentrated to achieve a red finish.

with a cutting wheel. Secure the top and bottom together with a little royal icing, allow to dry.

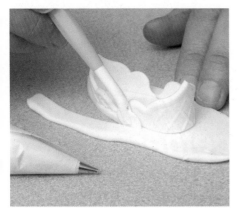

PME Pointers

When painting with food colour use a little clear alcohol to let the colours down, this will dry much more quickly than water and is less likely to eat into your icing.

13 Paint the squares on the side of the sledge with red and blue, then paint the outer edges and inner lines with gold.

14 Place Father Christmas into the sledge, positioning him towards the front, angled slightly so his face is visible. Secure with royal icing, fill the back of the sledge with small sweets.

15 Place the reindeer and the sledge onto the smallest cake and secure them with royal icing. Add a length of cotton to form the reins, put one end in Father Christmas' left hand then take the cotton down the row of reindeer to Rudolf at the end and bring it back up the other row of reindeer to the right hand.

16 Randomly place the trees onto top and the sides of the both cakes. Add a little royal icing to the top of the cake and board, sprinkle with glitter flakes, this will highlight the snow effect. Pipe snow onto the tops of the trees. Pipe a little snow at the base of the trees on the side of the cake.

17 Finish the board off with a ribbon, secured with double sided tape.

Romantic Engagement

This cake depicts the joining of two hearts and the start of a life together

by Christine Smith

1 Cover the board in mauve sugarpaste and leave to dry for 24 hours.

2 For a fruit cake, cover the cake with marzipan and leave to dry before coating with mauve sugarpaste. Allow a further 24 hours to dry.

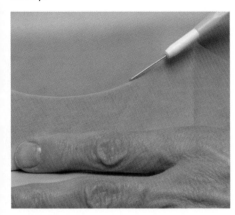

3 Measure the side of the cake from the pointed end of the heart to the centre of the rear indentation. Cut some greaseproof paper to this length and to three-quarters of the depth of the cake - fold into three lengthways. Mark scallops on the greaseproof paper to half the depth of the cake. Position the pattern against the side of the cake and mark the line with a scriber tool.

Checklist · Checklist · Checklist

- Cake - heart 25cm(10in)
- Heart shape cakeboard 31cm(12in)
- Sugarpaste 1.25Kg (2lb 8oz) mauve
- Flowerpaste 100g (4oz)
- Royal icing - small quantity
- Colour - violet
- Dusting powder - silver, pearlised white
- Ribbon for board
- Greaseproof paper
- Garrett frill cutter
- Scriber needle
- Fine basketweave rolling pin
- Carnation cutter large
- Stainless steel heart cutters
- Heart plunger cutter large
- Star from sweet pea set
- Closed curve crimper large - plain
- Open curve crimper small- plain
- Cutting wheels
- Bulbulous cone tool
- Ribbon tube 31R
- Wires - white 26 gauge
- Rolling pin small
- Paint brushes

4 Make a long narrow roll of sugarpaste about the thickness of a pencil. Moisten the bottom edge of the cake and attach the roll. Use a large plain closed curve crimper to pinch together as evenly as possible.

5 Colour approximately 100g (4oz) of sugarpaste dark mauve. Roll out thinly and use a garrett frill cutter, together with the largest centre, to cut out a circle.

6 Frill with the cone tool by holding firmly with a finger on

PME Pointers

To make a smooth even roll of sugarpaste, use a side scraper or smoother, rolling it backwards and forwards

the tool, roll the cone end backwards and forwards on each scallop. This will thin and frill the edge.

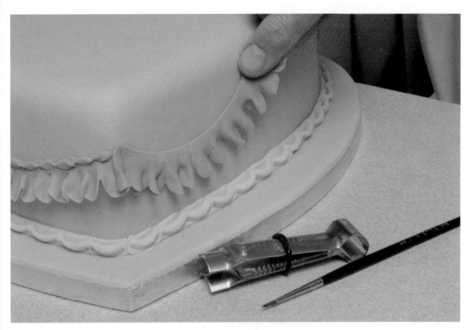

open curve crimper. This must be done before the paste dries out.

10 Roll out a small portion of dark mauve sugarpaste and texture with the fine basketweave rolling pin. Cut out six hearts using a medium size stainless steel cutter, cut out a further six hearts in pale mauve using the largest heart plunger cutter.

7 Cut the frilled circle and open out. Turn it over and moisten the top edge with water. Attach to the cake following the scalloped guideline, press firmly. To prevent the frill from falling against the cake, lightly brush the underside of the frill with the bristle end of a paintbrush.

8 Make more frills. To join the next section of frill and for neatness, fold the leading end under and butt up to the existing frill.

9 When all the frills are attached to the cake, crimp the top edge of the frill with a small plain

11 Dust the medium hearts with pearlised white powder and the smaller ones with silver powder. Attach a small heart on to larger one with royal icing. Place the hearts on each scallop peak securing with a dot of royal icing.

12 For the box, colour half the flowerpaste dark mauve. Roll out thinly and texture with a fine basketweave rolling pin. For the base and rim of the box, cut two scalloped circles with the largest carnation cutter. Cut out the centre of one circle using the central disc of the garrett frill.

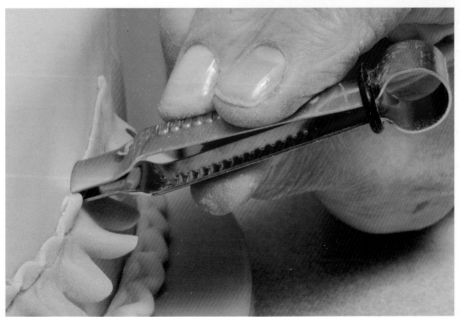

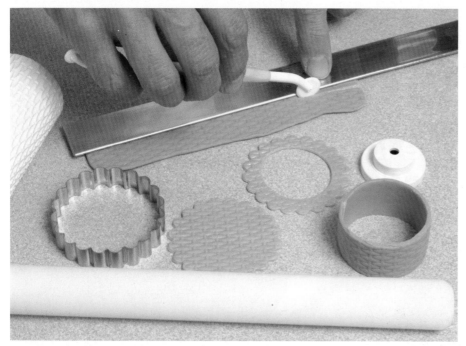

cushion in a random arrangement, varying their height.

19 Use a ribbon tube (31R) to pipe the 'congratulations' inscription in pale mauve royal icing. When dry, carefully paint with silver dusting powder mixed with a few drops of clear alcohol.

20 Use the fine basketweave rolling pin to texture a small piece of dark mauve sugarpaste and cut out a shape with the largest stainless steel heart cutter. Dust this with white pearlised powder. Roll out a small piece of pale mauve sugarpaste with a smooth rolling pin, with the same cutter cut out a heart. Remove a small section of the heart to allow the two hearts to nest together. Dust this heart with silver powder and place under the inscription securing it with royal icing. Add the board ribbon.

13 With the cutting wheel, cut out a textured strip measuring 15cm(6in) x 2.5cm(1in). Join each end together with royal icing and place around a 4cm(1.5in) round cutter for support - leave to dry.

14 Paint several wires silver and cut to various lengths. Wind a few wires around a pencil to create spirals.

17 When all three pieces for the box are dry, join the band to the base with a little royal icing. Mould a cushion of mauve sugarpaste and place it in the centre, then attach the rim to the top edge of the box. Dust the box with white pearlised powder.

18 Position the box on top of the cake and secure with royal icing. Insert the wired hearts, stars and spirals into the sugarpaste

15 Divide the remaining flowerpaste into four and colour each portion in varying shades of mauve. Roll out the paste and texture with a fine basketweave rolling pin then cut out a selection of three sizes of hearts and a few stars.

16 Moisten one end of the wire and carefully insert it into the pointed ends of the hearts and stars. Dust some with white pearlised powder and others silver.

A Modern Wedding

A wedding cake to capture the warmth and colour of the 21st century

by
Christine Smith

1 Cover the large cake drum with pink sugarpaste and leave to dry for 24 hours.

2 For rich fruit cakes, coat with marzipan and leave to dry for 24 hours. Place the tiers on single cake cards to match the size of the cakes. Sugarpaste the bottom tier in pink, the middle tier in yellow and the top tier in blue. Leave to dry for 24 hours.

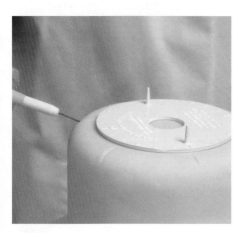

3 Use the cake marker on each tier, divide in to six equal sections and mark with the scriber needle the top and bottom edge. On the top tier mark a 4cm (1½in) circle in the middle.

4 Place the coated bottom tier onto the covered board. Cut three dowelling rods to the depth of the cake. Insert these into the cake in the shape of a triangle, not exceeding the size of the board for the middle tier. Repeat this procedure for the middle tier. Position the middle tier on the bottom tier and the top tier on to the middle one, ensuring dividing marks align.

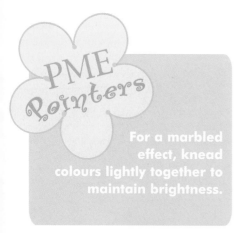

PME Pointers

For a marbled effect, knead colours lightly together to maintain brightness.

5 Roll out a small amount of pink sugarpaste and texture with the ribbed rolling pin. With the cutting wheel, cut six strips measuring 2cm(¾in) wide and long enough to go from the outer ring marking of the centre disc to the base of the top tier. Crimp the sides of each strip with the small plain closed scallop crimper. Moisten the back of the strip and attach to the cake, positioning it to the right hand side of each mark.

6 For the middle tier, roll out a small amount of blue sugarpaste and cut six strips long enough to stretch from the base of the top tier to the base of the middle tier. These should measure 2cm(¾in) wide increasing to 2.5cm (1in). Crimp the sides of the strips with the plain closed scallop crimper. Moisten the back of the strip and butt the narrow end to the base of the pink strip, angling the end slightly and laying the strip diagonally to the next bottom marker.

7 For the bottom tier make a further six textured strips using yellow sugarpaste measuring 2.5cm(1in) wide and long enough to reach the edge of the board.

PME Pointers

When using crimpers, position the 'O' ring for the desired depth and for eveness of pattern

8 To neaten the base of each tier, make thin rolls of sugarpaste using all three colours and twist together to make a single rope. Roll the multi coloured rope to the thickness of a pencil. On the top tier,

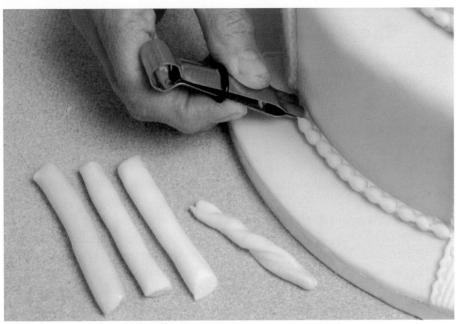

10 Roll out a small quantity of blue sugarpaste and cut out twenty four flowers with the second largest blossom plunger cutter. Place four evenly spaced on each yellow strip on the bottom tier. Finish by indenting the centre of the blossoms with the serrated cone tool. Repeat this for the top tier but with yellow blossoms on pink strips.

moisten the bottom edge of the cake between the strips and press the rope into place. Use a craft knife to trim the roll to the edge of each strip. Crimp the roll with the large plain open scallop crimper. Repeat this procedure for the middle and bottom tiers. Place a piece of multi-coloured rope around the 4cm(1½in) marked circle on the top tier, crimp to finish.

PME Pointers

To make a smooth even roll of sugarpaste, use a side scraper or smoother, rolling it backwards and forwards over the roll

9 Roll out a piece of blue sugarpaste 1.5 mm(1/16in) thick and cut out twelve bells using the larger bell shaped cutter. Crimp the bottom edge of each bell with the small plain closed scallop crimper. Moisten the back side edges of the bells and hang two side by side

in each section of the bottom tier, 1 cm (3/8in) from the top edge. Use the bulbulous cone tool to shape the bells into a curve away from the cake. For the top tier roll out yellow sugarpaste and proceed in the same way.

11 For the middle tier roll out some pink sugarpaste and cut out thirty blossoms using the largest plunger cutter. Moisten the back and attach five evenly spaced on each blue strip. To finish, roll out a little yellow sugarpaste and with the ribbed rolling pin, texture in a criss-cross pattern. Using no.18 piping tube cut out thirty circles for the blossom centres, moisten and attach.

12 Make four thin rolls of sugarpaste in each of the three colours and place side by side alternating the colours - moisten with

PME Pointers

To produce cupped shape flower blossoms press the plunger into foam sponge

water to stick together if necessary. Flatten with plain rolling pin and texture with the ribbed rolling pin in a criss-cross pattern. Use the cutting wheel across the colours to produce twelve ribbon tails 6cm(2½in) long and 1cm(⅜in) wide - cut the bottom edge at a slanting angle. For the bottom tier hang two tails just above each pair of bells, fix the top only to allow the tails to fall freely. Repeat for the top tier, slightly reducing the length and width of the tails.

13 With multi-coloured flattened and textured strips of sugarpaste cut six lengths of approximately 12cm(4½in) and 1cm (⅜in) wide. Take a strip and turn on its side and shape into three even loops, moisten at the base of each and pinch together - repeat this process for the other five sections. Allow to set firm and attach just above the ribbon tails on the bottom tier. Repeat for top tier but make loops slightly smaller.

14 For the top arrangement, mix a small quantity of flowerpaste to match each of the cake colours. Cut out some blossoms in each colour with the largest blossom cutter together with a few multi-coloured ones. When almost dry, pierce each centre with the scriber needle and when totally dry, insert white wires fixing with edible glue. Make the centres for the flowers in all three colours, use the other sizes of blossom cutters. When dry, use edible glue to fix one or two in varying sizes and colours, to the centre of each of the wired blossoms - finish by adding a dot of yellow royal icing to each centre.

15 Cut the wires to various lengths and arrange flowers in a flower pick. Insert the pick into the centre of the ring on the top tier. Disguise the top of the pick with a small quantity of the multi-coloured sugarpaste pressed around the base of the wires.

16 Glue a complementary colour ribbon around the edge of the cakeboard.

When using a scriber needle tool for centre of flowers, pierce into foam to avoid damaging work surfaces

Rocking Horse Christening Cake

By changing the colour scheme this charming christening cake will be suitable for a boy or girl

by Eileen Harper

1 Cover the board with ice blue sugarpaste and leave on one side to fully set (48 hours). Roll out the marzipan between spacers. Brush the cake with boiled sieved apricot jam and cover the cake with marzipan. Smooth the top and sides and trim away any surplus. Follow a similar procedure with pale melon sugarpaste brushing the marzipan this time with clear alcohol or cooled boiled water. Ensure there is a good finish to the cake by using the smoothers over the top and sides. Position the cake centrally on the board. Use piping tube no.5 and white royal icing to pipe around the base of the cake.

Checklist • Checklist • Checklist

- Fruit cake - hexagonal 25.5cm (10in)
- Marzipan - 1kg (2lb4oz)
- Sugarpaste pale melon - 1kg (2lb4oz)
- Sugarpaste ice blue - 500g (1lb2oz)
- Sugarpaste white - 500g (1lb2oz)
- Pastillage - 100g (4oz)
- Flowerpaste - 50g (2oz)
- Royal icing - 50g (2oz)
- Paste colour - ice blue, melon
- Powder colour - brown, primrose
- Cakeboard - hexagonal 36cm (14in)
- Marzipan spacers
- Smoothers
- Large rocking horse cutter
- Medium rabbit cutter
- Plaque cutter - 127mm
- Straight frill cutter
- Broderie anglaise eyelet cutters
- Bone modelling tool
- Scriber needle tool
- Bulbulous cone tool
- Designer wheel
- Craft knife
- Blossom plunger cutters
- Daisy marguerite plunger cutter
- Icing tubes no. 1.5, 5
- Icing bag and adaptor 20cm(8in)
- Ribbon for board edging 1¹/₂m

PME Pointers

Turn the pastillage items over periodically whilst drying to ensure that they dry flat.

PME Pointers

At this stage, if possible, leave the cake to 'skin' over for a couple of days. This will enable the cake to be worked on without leaving fingermarks.

3 From flowerpaste cut out twelve white daisies using the small daisy cutter. Press firmly with the embossing part of the cutter and this will give a raised centre to the daisy. With the bone modelling tool and working on a piece of soft foam or a flower pad, gently press each petal from the tip to the centre to give a more realistic curve to the flower.

4 For the broderie anglaise decoration, roll out a piece of white sugarpaste fairly thinly, big enough to cut out all six strips at once. Cut out six pieces, this ensures that they are all of a uniform thickness. Use the appropriate eyelet cutters to cut out the pattern shown. Until use, all strips should be covered with cling film or something similar to prevent drying out.

2 Use pastillage paste which has been coloured pale ice blue to cut out two of the large rocking horses. Colour some pastillage pale brown and cut out six large rabbits. Now cut out a plaque in white using the 127mm plaque cutter. Mark a raised pattern on each of the scallops using the round broderie anglaise eyelet cutter. Leave all these items to harden off.

PME Pointers

Pastillage is a paste containing edible gum that is suitable for plaques and simple cut-out shapes.

5 Use the end of the bulbulous cone tool to frill the bottom edge of the strip. Complete one strip at a time.

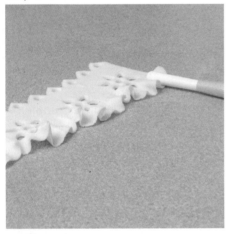

6 Dampen the underside of the strip with cooled boiled water and attach it to the cake. Repeat this procedure on all six sides.

7 For the corner bows, roll out some ice blue sugarpaste thinly and cut into strips measuring approximately 15x1cm(6x½in). Run the designer wheel along both side edges of the strip. Cut one piece a little longer than the other and cut out a 'v' shape at the end of each strip. Overlap each piece on the corner of the cake, ensuring that the join of the broderie anglaise strips is covered. Complete with the loops of a bow made in the same way and knotted with a further strip as shown in the picture.

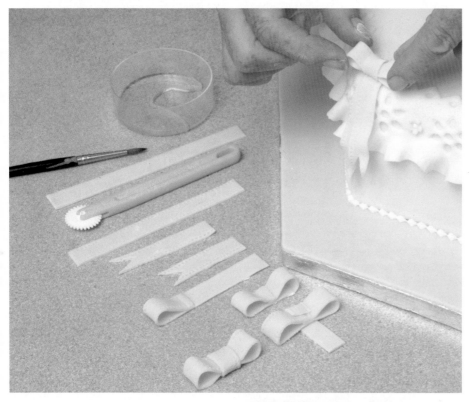

Leave to set, then brush with brown powder colour along the join of the mane.

9 To finish the cake attach the plaque in the middle of the cake slightly towards the back. Roll out some ice blue sugarpaste thinly and cut out some medium blossoms with the blossom ejector. Press a blossom directly onto the cake between each broderie anglaise cut out. Also place a blossom between each of the scallops on the plaque. With white royal icing and a no.1.5 piping tube, pipe a small dot in the centre of each blossom. Position a rabbit on top of the cake at each corner and add a white fluffy tail on each with royal icing and the no.5 piping tube.

Use primrose powder colour to carefully dust the centre of each daisy. Position three daisies either side of the plaque leaving space for the message. Place a daisy spaced evenly on each side of the cake below the frill

Pipe the message or name in ice blue royal icing and finish with a tiny dot at the top of each zig zag pattern on all the broderie anglaise pieces.

Complete the cake by adding the board edging ribbon.

8 To assemble the rocking horse, colour the rockers, tail and mane with brown powder colour. Put a few spots of colour on the rear of the horse and paint in the eye. Make a glue by diluting some of the ice blue pastillage with water. When dry this will blend in with the rest of the horse and not be noticed. Stick the two rocking horses together with the pastillage glue, spacing the rockers slightly apart.

Eastern Promise

This theme based on Moorish art has been inspired by the creative plaque embossing cutters, while the very elegant proportions of the cake are created by varying the height of the pillars.

A wedding cake by
Elaine MacGregor

See template pages on 114-115. Take a paper template from each cake tin as a pattern for the centre design and pillar position. Trace the rose patterns.

1 Cover each petal shaped cake with a thin layer of marzipan 5mm($\frac{1}{4}$in) and when dry, cover with sugarpaste, make sure that the indents and top edges are nicely rounded. Place each cake on its board. While the sugarpaste is still soft the centre top patterns need to be embossed. Mark the centre point of each cake and use a scriber to lightly mark faint lines across the cake from indent to indent (see diagrams).

For each cake use the appropriate sized cutter set in the "B" postition, line up with the scribed lines and press into the surface of the soft icing to emboss the patterns into the paste. Leave to dry. Dust the centre of each of the embossed patterns with lustre. Mix gold dusting powder with edible painting solution to form a gold paint and paint the embossed pattern edges. Leave to dry.

Checklist • Checklist • Checklist

- Cakes - petal shaped - 31,25,20,15cm (12,10,8,6in);
- Cakeboards -gold, petal shaped - 43,31,25,21cm (17,12,10,8$\frac{1}{2}$in)
- Cakeboard - round - 31cm (12in)
- Marzipan - 6$\frac{1}{2}$k (15lb)
- Sugarpaste - 6$\frac{1}{2}$k (15lb)
- Flowerpaste - white,green 250g (8oz) red, burgundy 125gm (4oz)
- Pastillage/flowerpaste - 680g (1$\frac{1}{2}$lb)
- Piping gel,sugar glue
- Confectioners' glaze
- Crystal-look pillars - three of each size - 18,12.5,8cm (7,5,3 in)
- Dowels - 9 cut to size (height of cake plus height of pillar)
- Ribbons - 3.5m x 13mm plain red for dowels; 4m each red and gold for cakeboard edges
- Dusting powders - poppy red, lemon yellow, moss green
- Lustre powder - gold, white, red
- Painting solution
- Paste colours - red, green, brown
- Royal icing
- Crimper sets - closed curve, closed scallop
- Creative plaque embossing cutters
- Five petal blossom cutters - set of 4
- Flower blossom X-Large plunger cutter
- Calyx cutters - set of 3
- Rose leaf plunger cutters
- Paint palettes
- Flower former sets
- Dimple foam sponge
- Bulbulous cone tool
- Veiner and scriber
- Ball and bone tools
- Paintbrushes - sable fine 0 and 000
- Paintbrushes - flat dusting
- No.42 tube and piping bags
- Tracing paper

2 Work on one tier at a time. With sugarpaste, cut out and emboss six appropriately sized shapes ('A' stop embosser, 'B' stop

cutter). Gild the edges of each piece, dust over with lustre. Cut three of the shapes horizontally in half.

With the sugarpaste still pliable paint the back of the cut piece with glue and position one half of the cut piece on the side of the cake (cut edge touching the board). Bend the other half slightly to accommodate the curve, matching up the points, and attach to the covered cakeboard.

PME Pointers

Place the three other uncut shapes within the indent of the petal shape, bend the top point slightly, so that it matches the point of the embossed pattern on the top surface of the cake.

Required for each cake - including centre "lotus flower"	Base	Tier 2	Tier 3	Tier 4	Total
Briar roses - large	4	3			7
Briar roses - medium	6	6	6	3	21
Briar roses - small	12	4	4	1	21
Briar roses - very small	6	9	9	9	33
Briar roses - buds	15	12	15	12	54
Rose leaves - large	6				6
Rose leaves - medium	12	6	6	6	30
Rose leaves - small	18	12	12	9	51
Pastillage off pieces - X large	6				6
Pastillage off pieces - large	6	6			12
Pastillage off pieces - medium	6	6	6		18
Pastillage off pieces - small			6	6	12

3 Trace the rose patterns from the pattern pages and scribe them onto the cakes. Use very fine sable brushes and paste colours to paint the patterns onto the cake sides and the board edge of the base tier. Use royal icing and a no.42 tube to pipe a line of shells around the base of each cake.

The flowers and leaves

4 With green flowerpaste and the large and medium calyx cutters, cut the shapes and place in a palette to form into a curve. Use white flowerpaste and the three

largest of the blossom cutters to cut the flowers. Frill the edges of each flower with a bulbulous cone tool, cup the petals with a ball tool and use the veiner to mark the centre veins. Paint sugar glue onto the prepared calyx and attach the flower, lining up the calyx points to the centre of each petal. Leave to dry.

5 Small and very small flowers are made with a double layer of flowerpaste. Roll out the red

paste, then the same amount of white paste. Place the white over the red and roll out the two layers together, the layers will adhere. Cut out using the small blossom cutter and the large plunger cutter, frill the edges with the cone tool, place on a green calyx and indent into a piece of dimple foam to form tighter flowers.

For the rose buds, roll a small pea sized piece of red paste into a cone, thin one side to form into a petal and wrap that around the cone. Cut a small green calyx, paint with sugar glue, place the wider end of the cone into the centre, wrap the calyx points up the sides of the cone. Leave to dry.

6. When the larger white flowers are dry, brush the insides with a light dusting of pale lemon dusting colour. To prevent any red colour from dropping into the centre of the flower, place a small piece of cotton wool inside the flower, then use a dry dusting brush and red dust to colour the edges of the petals. Remove the cotton wool, paint a small spot of flowerpaste glue into the centre of the flower and place a very small ball of yellow paste over it, indent with a scriber to give the impression of stamens.

7. The rose leaves are made using a double layer of burgundy and green coloured flowerpaste. Cut a selection of the three sizes (see chart). Dust with various green dusts. Glaze with confectioners' glaze, remove the surplus on a paper towel, then twist into shape and leave to dry on foam sponge.

8. Assemble the flowers onto the painted backgrounds securing with royal icing.

Lotus Shapes

9. Use creative plaque embossing cutters ('A' stop on the embosser with the 'B' stop on the cutter) to cut the appropriate number of pastillage pieces for each tier (see chart). Lift each cut piece and drop

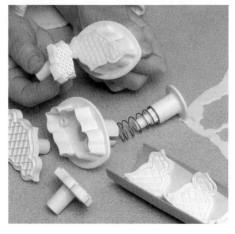

back into the cutter, then use the alternate embosser supplied with the set to press it into the well of the cutter, thus embossing the pastillage piece on both sides. Gently lift off the embosser, placing the pastillage piece in a flower former tray to achieve the curve. Leave to dry. Dust both sides of the each piece with lustre, paint the inside edges with red paste colour and gild the outside edges. Leave the paint to dry.

Assembly of Lotus shapes

10. Paint sugar glue on the centre of the cake. Form some sugarpaste into a ball, flatten this onto the cake. Start with the largest cut pieces, assemble six pieces between the six patterns embossed into the top of the cake. A small amount of royal icing may be used to secure.

11. Once the first layer is in position, assemble six smaller pastillage pieces in the gaps formed by the first layer. On the first or base tier, there are three rows of cut pastillage pieces, on the two middle tiers, there are two rows, and on the top tier, only one row.

PME Pointers

To achieve the red glow through the crystal pillar wrap red ribbon round the visible part of the pillar.

12. Royal icing is used to secure the flowers and leaves in position in the centre of the 'Lotus' shape, making sure that no gaps are left unadorned.

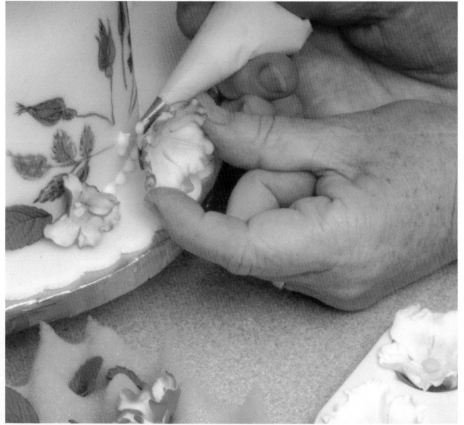

Marzipan and Almond Paste

This paste has been traditionally used for coating rich fruit cakes prior to covering with royal icing or sugarpaste. In addition the natural almond flavour and firm texture make it ideal for modelling and decorating.

In many countries around the world almond pastes are extremely popular and used to decorate gateaux, torten, sweets and fillings for dried fruits. Also modelled figures and flowers are often created with this paste.

A range of commercial almond pastes is readily available in a variety of different qualities. The main difference being in the proportion of almonds or nuts to sugar and the choice of white or yellow colour. These commercial pastes have the advantage of a much longer shelf life than home made paste.

Almond Paste

ground almonds 250g(8oz)
caster sugar 125g(4oz)
icing sugar - sifted 125g(4oz)
egg white 50g(2oz)

1 Place all of the dry ingredients into a bowl and stir together until well blended.

2 Make a well in the centre and gradually add in the egg white until a firm soft dough is achieved.

3 Yellow food colour can be added if required.

4 Place in an air tight plastic bag.

5 The sugars can be replaced with soft dark brown sugar for a richer taste.

6 Liquid almond essence may be added to increase the flavour.

PME Pointers

Always use icing sugar for dusting when coating as this will give the cake a longer shelf life and help protect against possible fermentation problems.

PME Pointers

Almond paste can easily be coloured using concentrated paste or jel colours, but remember that the natural colour of the paste will affect the finished results.

To cover a cake for Royal Icing

Whether the cake has been home made or commercially produced each cake will be different and therefore the preparation may vary.

1 Begin by turning the cake upside down and placing onto a cake board.

2 Fill any gaps at the base of the cake by rolling out a sausage shape of almond paste and firmly pushing it into the spaces. Trim the paste so that it is flush with the cake.

3 If there are any holes in the cake surface that may affect the final finish, fill them with small pieces of almond paste.

4 **Sides** - Use icing sugar for dusting. Roll out a strip of almond paste slightly wider than the height of the cake. To achieve an even thickness of paste, place marzipan/sugarpaste spacers either side of the paste as it is rolled out.

5 Measure the height of the cake and trim the paste to fit.

6 To attach the almond paste to the cake, either spread a very thin layer of boiled sieved apricot jam onto the paste or

alternatively brush the cake with the jam, the paste can be attached in sections if required.

7 **Top** - Roll out the almond paste to a shape similar to the cake, but slightly larger, again use the spacers and icing sugar for dusting.

8 Brush the top of the cake with a thin layer of boiled sieved apricot jam. Invert the cake onto the almond paste and press down firmly. Trim the paste with a knife, turn the cake back up the right way again and replace onto the cake board.

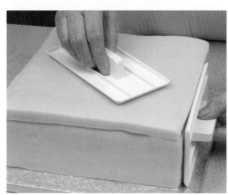

9 Use two smoothers to polish the surface, ensuring that any blemishes etc. are removed. Place to dry overnight.

To cover a cake for coating with sugarpaste.

To prepare the cake for coating with sugarpaste or as a final cake coating with a soft finish to the cake edges, cover the cake in one piece. The cake can be used either up the right way or turned over and prepared as for royal icing.

1 Brush the cake with boiled sieved apricot jam.

2 Use icing sugar for dusting. Roll out the almond paste to a similar shape to the cake. The paste should be slightly larger than required to cover both the top and sides. Use the marzipan/sugarpaste spacers to ensure an even thickness.

3 Polish the surface of the paste with a smoother to remove any blemishes and excess icing sugar.

4 Place the rolling pin across the centre of the paste and carefully wrap the paste over the pin. Lift up the pin and transfer the almond paste to evenly cover the cake.

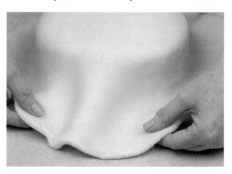

5 Use the side of the hands to ease the paste into position. If coating a cake with corners concentrate on the corners first, gently cupping the paste in place.

6 Remove any folds or gathers by gently stretching the paste out at the base of the cake. Trim the excess paste away with a knife.

7 Use the smoothers to polish the surface and remove any blemishes. Place to dry overnight.

Marzipan Modelling

by Nadene Hurst

Marzipan has texture and handling properties that lend themselves to caricature figures, this can be lots of fun!

1 When using a non-stick rolling pin and board it should not be necessary to use any other medium to prevent sticking. However icing sugar can be used, but only sparingly, as it may spoil the surface appearance of the marzipan. Never use cornflour, it causes the marzipan to ferment.

2 Paste colours or colour-flavours are the most suitable for colouring marzipan. As the natural colour of marzipan is not white and there are instances where pure white is desirable, such as for eyes, small amounts of sugarpaste can be used.

3 Glazing is unnecessary if the models are to be used and eaten within a short period. Water or stock syrup will give a temporary glaze, but if long term storage is required commercial glazes are available, to be brushed on or sprayed.

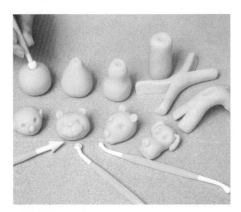

4 Every part of a model begins with a ball shape, this smoothes out any creases and cracks on the surface. This is important because they will open as the marzipan dries out and spoil the appearance.

5 To commence modelling, divide the model into the basic shapes. For bodies, a ball, cone, pear and/or roll. For heads , a ball, oval, cone or pear shape. Most arms and legs start off as cones of varying thickness and length. Combinations of these can produce all sorts of figures and animals.

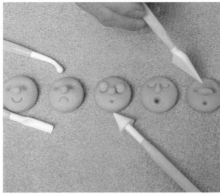

6 Expressions can be achieved in simple ways. Use the scallop tool in opposite directions, curving up for happy and down for sad. For asleep fill the eye sockets with marzipan balls and indent below them with the scallop tool, finish with a small cone shaped hole for the mouth.

7 To denote someone singing, place a ball of paste in the mouth position, then impress deeply with the cone tool. The eyes can be open or closed. To show worry or anger, impress wavy lines across the forehead with the blade tool, and add a small cone shaped hole for the mouth.

8 Hairstyles add character. A strip round the centre of the head, impressed with vertical lines, makes a good bald head. For a full head of hair cut out a circle of paste, attach and impress radiating lines all round.

Overlapping circles can create interesting styles with the addition of a bun on the top, or one on each side. Curly hair is made by pressing some marzipan through a sieve, and plaits are made by twisting two thin rolls of paste together.

9 Shapes from the rollerboards can also be used. See how the pear shape has been used for the rabbit's body and the pig's head. The strawberry shape has been used for the pig's and the frog's bodies.

10 A teddy bear is easily made from a cone body, indented at the top with a large ball tool. Add a ball shaped head, with a flattened roll for the muzzle. Indent with a cone for the eyes and nose, and fill with black cone shapes.

The ears are two balls, indented and pressed into position with the bone tool. The arms and legs are long cones, shaped as shown and pressed onto the side of the body. Finish with stitches using the small stitch wheel.

11 To make the dog start with four cone shapes, impressed at the wide ends with the shell tool. Arrange them as shown and flatten down the centre. Make the body with a large cone, place on top of the legs and indent on both sides with the blade tool to form the back legs.

Make the head from a short roll, narrowed across the centre into a dumbbell shape. Add the ears, nose, mouth and tail into holes made with the cone tool. The ears and the tongue are flattened cones of marzipan.

12 For the Santa make an even roll of red paste and indent at each side with the bone tool, holding the ball end at the top. This makes grooves for the arms to rest in. Add a strip of plain marzipan round the base and impress with vertical lines. Make two arms from cones and place them on the sides of the body.

Roll a flesh coloured ball for the head, add features, then a beard, hair and moustache. Make the hat from a cone, with the broad end flattened to fit on the head. Add a bobble on the hat, buttons and mittens to complete.

13 The snowman's body is a cone, painted with edible glue, and rolled in caster sugar. Make two indents on the sides and add ball shapes for arms. Another ball makes the head, again rolled in caster sugar. Add a strip of red paste for the scarf, and two flattened balls of black to make the hat. Complete with eyes and a 'carrot' nose.

Fruit Basket
An edible feast

An edible feast - the firm, but malleable, consistency of marzipan lends itself to modelling in many forms. A patterned rolling pin and rollerboards make it easy to produce these attractive items quickly and easily.

by Nadene Hurst

Two different grades of marzipan are used in the decoration of this cake. One type is normally used to cover cakes, then there is a modelling marzipan to make the fruits - this is a finer quality and contains glucose.

1 Colour 100g(4oz) of covering marzipan green, and use to cover the cakeboard. Leave to dry for at least twenty four hours.

2 Level the top of the cake and brush with boiled apricot jam. Roll out some natural coloured marzipan to 5mm ($1/4$in) thick and cover the top of the cake. With the cake upside-down, fill in any gaps on the top corners with marzipan to form a flat top for the basket. Madeira cake always bakes with a domed top, if this is all removed the cake would be too shallow, so a little ajustment is necessary. Turn the cake the right way up.

3 Colour 600g(1lb4oz) of marzipan brown. Roll out to 5mm($1/4$in) thickness then roll over with the basketweave rolling pin. Measure the width of each side of the cake at the top and bottom, as the shape narrows towards the base and cut out the two end pieces first. Attach these with apricot jam.

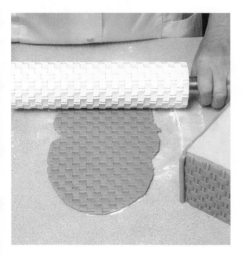

4 Cut out the two side pieces and attach them to the cake. With some of the remaining marzipan make a narrow roll, about 5mm($1/4$in) thick, to cover each corner join.

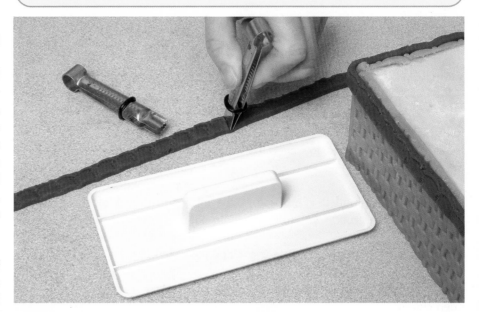

5 Add extra colouring to the remainder of the brown marzipan, making it a much deeper shade. Make a 1cm($1/2$in) roll, then flatten slightly using a smoother. Crimp along one edge with the closed scallop crimper, then in between the scallops with the straight one. Attach this strip all round the top of the cake.

6 Repeat the process to make the handle, but crimp down both edges this time. Drape the handle round one end of the basket and attach the ends half way along the top edge with edible glue. Trim if necessary.

7 Place the cake onto the green covered cakeboard, slightly nearer to one edge, to leave extra space at the front.

PME Pointers

Do not make the cover for the cake until the fruits are ready. If the cover is soft it will be easier to arrange the fruit, and push it into the folds.

8 Roll out an oblong of natural marzipan. Colour 90g(3oz) of marzipan blue and roll out thinly into a square. Cut into strips and lay across the top of the natural paste in a check pattern. Roll diagonally with a small rolling pin to press the pattern into the background.

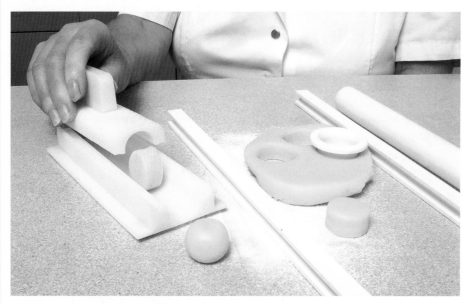

9 Cut into a neat square, approximately 20cm(8in), and drape on the cake making folds on the top. Do not allow it to fall too far down the sides to cover the basketweave.

10 Colour the modelling marzipan for the fruits as follows:

100g(4oz) each of green and pale egg yellow.
50g(2oz) of orange, lemon, red and deep claret.
25g(1oz) of brown.

11 Roll out the paste between the spacers provided. Cut out several discs with the cutter provided. When using the round shape rollerboard place the marzipan discs lengthways, as shown, in the bottom half. Place the top half over the marzipan, locate into the channels at the sides, and slide backwards and forwards to form a ball. The ball shape is used for apples, peaches, plums and oranges.

12 When using the appropriate rollerboards to produce lemons, pears and strawberries the marzipan disc is placed sideways into the rollerboard channel, before proceeding in the same way as already described.

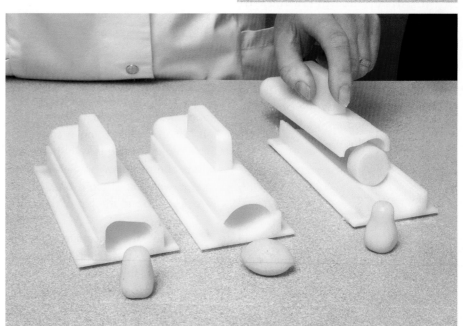

13 **Oranges and lemons**
After forming the oranges and lemons, gently roll them on a metal sieve for a textured surface. Use a plain cone tool to indent both ends of the lemons. A touch of green colouring on one end of a lemon adds interest. Place a tiny ball of brown paste on top of the oranges, and press in with a serrated cone.

14 **Apples and pears**
Use light green marzipan. To complete the apples indent gently on the top with the large ball tool, then make a hole with the plain cone. Insert a tiny stalk into the hole and add a leaf at one side. Treat the pears in the same way, but cut out a tiny brown star shape, place on the bottom and press in with the cone. Finish both fruits with a touch of red

and/or green down one side for a realistic effect.

Peach

15 Roll a pale yellow ball shape. Using the back of the blade tool indent a line down one side, starting with the thickest end at the top. Make a hole with the cone tool at the top of the line. A stalk is optional. Add a blush of red on one side.

Plums

16 Use the deep claret colour and shape in the same way as the peach, but add a stalk. To finish add a touch of black on one side.

Strawberries and Pineapple

17 Shape the strawberries, in red, and pineapples, in yellow, from the same rollerboard. Paint the strawberries with beaten egg white or edible glue and dip them in caster sugar. Make a large indent on the top with the ball tool. Cut out a green calyx and press it in the top with a cone tool.

18 To make the calyx for the pineapples mix together some green and brown paste for a mottled effect. Cut out two calyx for each fruit and alternate them on top. Press in the centre with the serrated cone. Carefully indent all round the fruit with the same cone to make a knobbly appearance.

Caricatures

19 To add features to the fruits, indent with a bone tool for the eyes. Fill these in with tiny balls of white sugarpaste, press in another hole with the small ball tool and fill this with black for the pupil. Arms are small rolls of brown paste inserted into holes made with a plain cone. Legs or feet can be laid underneath the fruit.

20 To finish the cake arrange the fruits on top, take advantage of the folds in the cover to hold them in place. If any will not stick use edible glue to secure them. A few fruits on the board adds interest, also patches of extra green marzipan, marked with a shell tool, and a few blossom flowers.

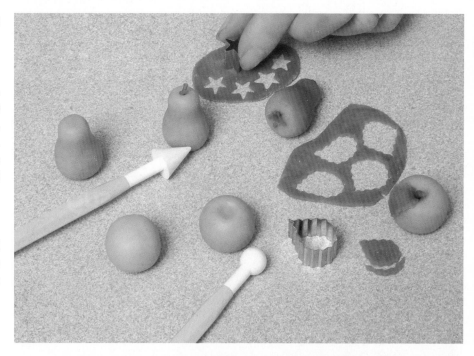

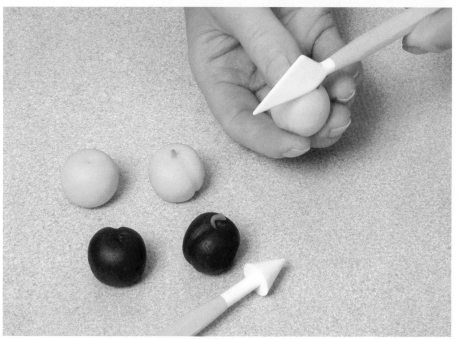

Marzipan Floral Cake

This quick to decorate cake uses marzipan paste for the decorative effect and is suitable as an alternative to sugarpaste

by Eileen Harper

1 Measure the length and width of the cake and add approximately 2.5cm(1in) extra all round to the measurement. Roll out the marzipan between marzipan spacers to ensure an even thickness, keep measuring the piece until you have the required size. Paint the cake with melted apricot jam then carefully lift the marzipan with the aid of the rolling pin and position over the cake, make sure it is even all the way round. Gently pat the marzipan onto the cake and use the smoother to ensure a good finish.

Checklist • Checklist • Checklist

- ☐ Fruit cake - oval 20cm (8in)
- ☐ Marzipan - 1½k(3lb 5oz)
- ☐ Royal icing -100g(4oz)
- ☐ Dusting powder - gooseberry, primrose, fuchsia, lavender, spring green, gold. pearl white
- ☐ Rejuvenator spirit
- ☐ Cakeboard - oval 28cm(11in)
- ☐ Cakeboard - oval 30cm(12in)
- ☐ Marzipan spacers
- ☐ Smoother
- ☐ Cutting wheel
- ☐ Shell modelling tool
- ☐ Veining tool
- ☐ Bone modelling tool
- ☐ Ivy leaf plunger cutter small
- ☐ Blossom plunger cutters - set of 4
- ☐ Blossom plunger cutter
- ☐ Piping tube no.1.5
- ☐ Piping bag and adaptor - 20cm(8in)
- ☐ Selection of paintbrushes
- ☐ Ribbon for board edging

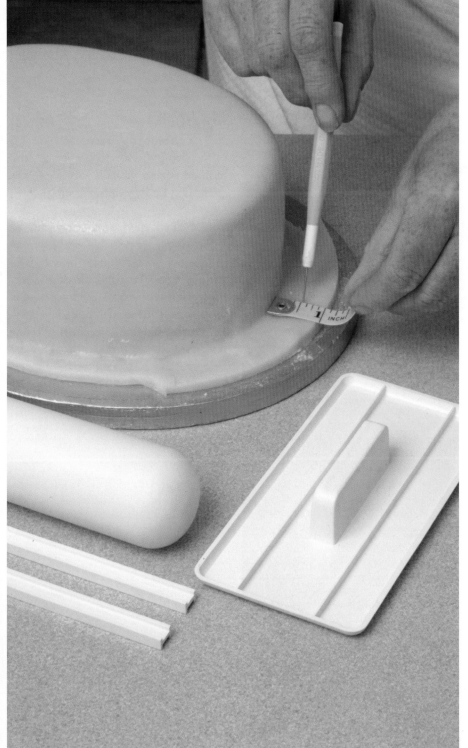

2 Ensure the marzipan fits tightly to the cake around the base and then use a tape measure to mark 1cm(½in) all the way round. Trim off any surplus with the cutting wheel.

3 While the paste is still soft press all the way round with the shell modelling tool. Use the veining tool to mark in a series of stems starting from the left hand side and sweeping down the right hand side towards the board.

PME Pointers Dip the shell modelling tool into a little icing sugar after each press to ensure it does not stick to the soft marzipan. Any surplus icing sugar can be gently brushed off when the marzipan has hardened.

4 Following the line of stems already marked on the cake, randomly press and emboss ivy leaves with the small ivy leaf plunger cutter into the surface of the marzipan. Mix some pearl white powder colour with rejuvenator spirit and paint the ivy leaves.

5 Use royal icing coloured pale gooseberry green and a no.1.5 icing tube to pipe in the marked stems (this is optional, the stems can be left without piping).

6 Roll out some marzipan as thinly as possible and then cut out a selection of blossoms in various sizes. Turn the blossoms over onto a foam pad and press each petal in turn with the bone modelling tool. Return the blossoms to the right side and gently brush on various powder colours. Leave some of the flowers without colour to add contrast.

PME Pointers

To give a soft translucent effect brush over the coloured blossoms and leaves with a small amount of pearl white powder colour.

PME Pointers

Press the plunger cutter into a little icing sugar periodically to help eject the pieces.

9 Arrange the blossoms and leaves onto the cake to give the impression of flowers tumbling down the right hand side onto the board. Attach the flowers and leaves with a small amount of royal icing. Pipe royal icing into the blossom centres.

10 Attach the larger gold oval board to the base of the finished cake to create a step effect. The board edges may be decorated with a pretty co-ordinating ribbon if required.

7 To vary the style of the blossoms place some of the smaller flowers into the centre of larger ones.

8 Mix some moss green powder into a small amount of marzipan and roll out very thinly. With the small ivy plunger cutter cut out and emboss some leaves.

Royal Icing Skills

The elegant beauty of a well produced royal iced cake is a delight to the cake decorator's eye

Royal Icing Recipe

- Water - 315ml(10fl oz)
- Albumen powder - 45g(1$\frac{1}{2}$oz)
- Icing sugar - 1.75 kg(3$\frac{1}{2}$lb)

Method

1 Dissolve the albumen powder in the water (see notes below), strain through a fine sieve, then re-measure to 315ml(10fl oz).

2 Place the liquid in a clean, fat- free, mixing bowl, add the icing sugar and stir to combine the ingredients.

3 Beat on an electric mixer, set to the slowest speed, until it reaches the required consistency. Beating times will vary according to the speed of the individual machine, but will be between four and six minutes.

Soft peak

Soft peak is the first consistency reached during beating, at approximately four minutes, and is used for the first coat on the cake and piping with writing tubes. When lifted from the bowl with a spatula, soft peak icing will retain a peak, but it will bend over at the tip.

Full peak

Full peak is a stiffer, firmer consistency, leaving a definite peak when lifted, and will not fall when shaken. Used for decorative piped borders that need to retain their patterned shapes. Softer consistency can be made up to full peak by returning to the mixer and beating for longer, never add extra icing sugar, it will cause the icing to dry extremely hard.

Storage

To avoid a crust forming on the icing, cover the bowl with a slightly damp cloth whilst working. Store in an airtight container with cling film (plastic wrap) pressed on to the surface of the icing. It is not necessary to store it in a refrigerator. The icing should be re-beaten on a mixer at least every two days, making the icing much easier to work.

Albumen (egg white) Powders

Powdered egg white is recommended for making royal icing, it complies with food safety standards and gives consistent results. The ability to accurately measure the ingredients makes royal icing simple to produce. Consistency can be difficult with fresh egg whites due to the variation in egg sizes and the water content.

The powders are available either as pure albumen, slightly yellow in colour, or as albumen substitutes, creamy white in colour. Substitutes are much cheaper and can be used for most tasks. Pure albumen powder is stronger and should be used when working on delicate designs.

Both need to be dissolved in water, the substitutes will mix almost immediately, but the pure type needs to be soaked for a while before it will dissolve.

Icing sugar

Icing sugar is sold in different grades, the finest being "bride cake". Coarse grades will need sieving, but the quality of many sugars makes this un-necessary, so it is worth experimenting to eliminate this arduous task. Try to avoid icing sugar containing cornflour, which causes the icing to lose its aeration quickly. If there is no alternative you will need to re-beat the icing every day.

Additions

Glycerine will prevent the icing from drying too hard and making it difficult to cut. Add between a half and one teaspoon to every 500g(1lb) of icing just before use. Never add glycerine to icing that will be used to make run-outs, it will prevent them from drying out. When colour is required always use liquid colour they will mix in easily without causing streaks. For large amounts weigh out an amount of icing and add a number of drops of colour. If you note this ratio you will be able to repeat the colour strength accurately when mixing the next batch.

Coating

Three coats of icing should be applied to a marzipan coated cake for a satisfactory finish, leaving the cake to dry completely between each coat.

Use soft peak icing for the first coat, add a small amount of water to soften the icing slightly for the second coat, then soften again for the final coat.

Top coating a round or square cake

Place the cake on a turntable, put a relevant amount of royal icing in the centre of the cake and paddle with a flat palette knife. Start in the centre and gradually work outwards.

Keep the knife at right-angles to the edge of the cake, at the same time working the icing backwards and forwards applying pressure, without taking the knife out. Turn the cake at the same time so that the knife takes the icing all across the cake. The paddling eliminates the air bubbles as well as spreading the icing. Remove the excess icing from the edge of the cake before proceeding.

Remove the cake from the turntable and place it on a flat work surface. Draw a straight edge over the top of the cake in one continuous movement to create a smooth surface.

When the top coat is dry, smooth the edges with a sharp knife to remove any lumps and bumps before coating the sides.

Side coating a round cake.

Place the cake on a turntable and paddle the icing on to the side a little at a time. Hold the palette knife vertically and position your index finger down the back of the blade to apply pressure. Rotate the cake and paddle the icing as you work. When the cake is completely covered, paddle all round the cake once again to form an even thickness and remove any excess from round the top and bottom edges. **N.B.** left handed people work in the oppostie direction.

Hold the side scraper in one hand and stretch your turning arm diagonally across the top of the cake to grip the cakeboard and turntable. Place the side scraper just in front of where you are holding the cakeboard and draw it round the cake until it almost reaches the front, pulling it off towards you to finish. At the same time revolve the turntable at a faster pace to compensate for the distance travelled by the scraper. This will leave a "take off" mark which can be removed later when the coating is dry. Neaten the top edge of the cake and round the base before leaving it to dry.

Side coating on a square cake

Paddle the icing on the side of the square cake in the same way as the round one, making sure that the corners are well covered. To smooth the first side, position the scraper slightly before the corner, bringing it on to the icing gently to avoid skinning the corner. Draw the scraper along and pull off towards yourself. Avoid pressing into the corner. Leave any excess icing down the corner, this will be removed when smoothing the next side.

Start the second side in the same way as the first, this will bring the 'take-off' mark from the first side round the corner as you start smoothing. Repeat this process until all four sides are coated. Ensure that all the edges are neat and clean before leaving to dry. Leave the final 'take-off' mark to be removed later when dry.

'Take off' marks

Remove these by scraping carefully with a craft knife. If the icing is coloured it will leave a lighter mark, remove this by painting with a slightly damp paintbrush. It is very important

to remove any unwanted icing, this can catch on the side scraper and spoil the next coat.

Coating a cake board

This can be done in two ways. The quicker and easier method is to leave the board until you have finished the final side coating, then, while the icing is still wet, coat the board with soft icing, resembling thick run sugar consistency.

Spread sufficient icing round the board with a small palette knife, then smooth gently without removing any of the icing. Trim round the edge of the board and leave to settle and dry. On a square board, smooth the icing from edge to edge on each side, which means that you are overlapping on the corners.

For a superior finish the boards can be coated separately from the cakes. Smaller boards can be coated all the way across, like the top of a cake. Larger boards should be coated with a 8cm(3in) band round the edge. These will require three coats like the cakes.

Coat the cakes on temporary boards, placing a thin cake card under the cake, the same size and shape as the cake. This thin card shold be left under the cake during coating and when it is transferred to the final board to avoid staining from the fruit cake, and the cake becoming sticky underneath. The cake can be removed from the temporary board by scoring round the base with a craft knife and pulling gently off.

Piping Techniques

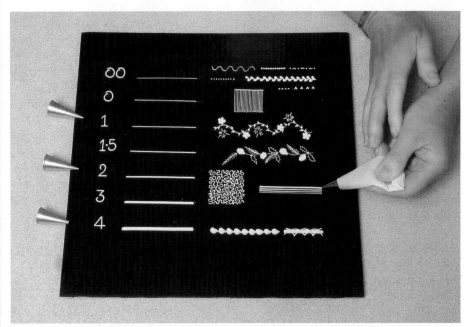

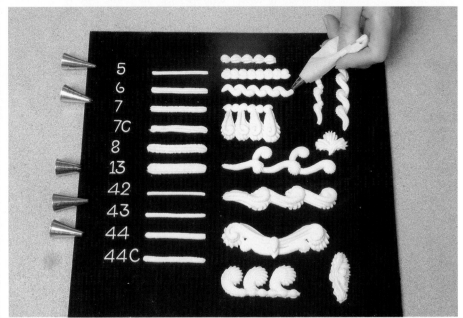

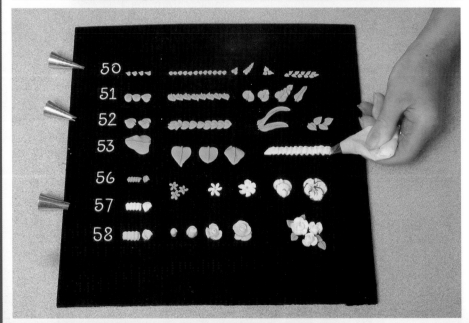

Writing tubes - 00, 0, 1, 2, 3, and 4
The common use is for writing on cakes and piping linework. Other uses are cornelli work, embroidery and fine borders. The larger ones are for piping bulbs or pearls round the base of a cake. Run-outs are outlined with a no.0 or 1 and extension work piped with a no. 00 or 0. Always paddle the icing before using it in a writing tip, this removes large air bubbles which can break the line as you are piping.

Star tubes - 5, 6, 7, 8 and 13
Rope tubes - 42, 43 and 44
Star and rope tubes are similar and can be interchanged for many uses. The difference is that the star tubes have fewer points, indicated by the tip number. Rope tubes, although similar in diameter to the star tubes, have more points and produce a finer effect. All are available with open and closed points, the closed ones being indicated by a 'C' after the number. There is a marked difference between the two effects produced.
These tubes are used mainly for borders, from the simple shell and star, up to elaborate overpiped patterns, which are usually combined with other types of tubes, particularly writing ones. Because they use a lot of icing it is advisable to use a fabric bag and adaptor.

Leaf tubes - 51, 52 and 53
These have two sets of indents on opposite sides. The smaller indents make the centre vein of the leaf. When piping, hold the piping bag so that the larger indents are on the sides, to form the leaf.

Petal tubes - 56, 57 and 58
These tubes are tapered in shape and curved to form cupped petals. They are the only tubes that are available in left and righthanded versions, to allow for each piping the opposite way round, and they are marked 'L' or 'R' after the number. Small frill effects and borders can be piped, and are particularly attractive when combined with scrolls.

A variety of flowers can be piped flat on a flower nail, and roses on a cocktail stick or moulded centre.

Piping requires accurate control of pressure and movement, and depending on the tubes used, you will require a suitable bag. When piping with larger tubes it is advisable to use a large, washable bag, fitted with an adaptor. As these are generally used for piping borders the adaptor makes it easier to change tubes as required.

For smaller tubes paper bags are used, holding the bag in one hand and supporting with a finger from the other. This results in greater control and accuracy. Illustrated here are the most commonly used icing tubes, grouped together where there is a similarity, to show a variety of uses.

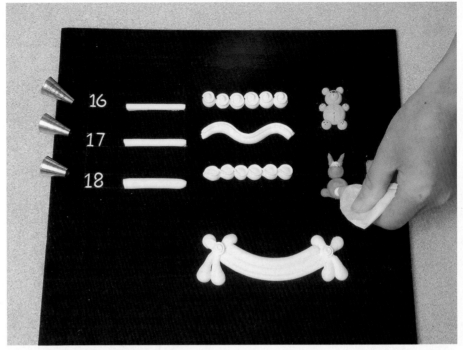

Pressure piping - 16, 17 and 18
These can be used to pipe large pearl borders, in the same way as a shell border, or ropes round the top or bottom of a cake. Straight, piped lines can be overpiped with contrasting tubes. Large bulbs can be combined to produce small figures and animals. Another handy use is as small, round cutters, when working with marzipan or paste.

Basketweave - 19B and 20B
These are small and medium sized tubes, used for traditional basketweave effects. You can pipe directly on to a cake or, alternatively, pipe to a pattern placed under run-out film, and trim the edges to the required shape whilst the icing is still wet.

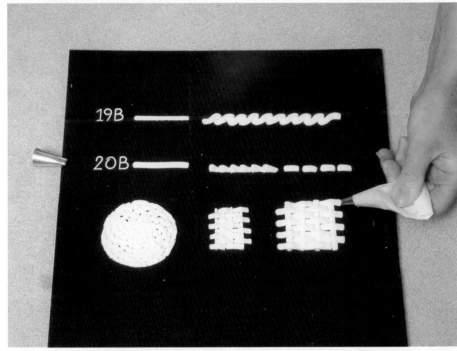

Ribbon tubes - 30R, 31R and 32R
These are flat ended, extruding a flat, straight line of varying widths depending on the size. Usually they are used to pipe lines of threaded ribbon of different widths with varying gaps between. They can be combined in borders with other tubes and flowers, and used to pipe small bows.

Calligraphy - 23, 24 and 25
These are similar in shape to the ribbon tubes, but much smaller. Combined with writing tubes, they are used to pipe a similar effect to written calligraphy. It is time consuming because of the constant changing of tubes.

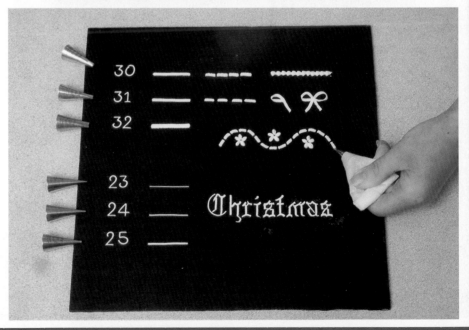

Birthday Celebration

A special birthday deserves a very special cake, a wonderful exercise in piping, this one cannot fail to impress.

by

Nadene Hurst

See pattern pages for templates

1 Glue the 30cm(12in) and 33cm(13in) boards together. Fill in the area round the edge with a slope of royal icing. Paddle the icing into the space, then smooth off with a small palette knife. Continue to coat the top of the board and the slope alternatively, in the same way as the top and sides of a cake, until you have obtained a good finish.

2 Marzipan the cake and slide a 23cm (9in) cake card underneath. This remains in position throughout the coating and assembly of the cake. Place on a spare cake board. Apply at least three coats of icing to the top and sides.

Checklist • Checklist • Checklist

- Fruit cake - round 23x11cm (9x4½in)
- Cakeboards - round 30cm(12in), 33cm(13in)
- Cake card - round 23cm(9in)
- Marzipan - 1.5kg(3 lb)
- Royal icing - cream 2kg(4 lb)
- Gum tragacanth
- Dusting powder - gold
- Alcohol
- Tilting turntable
- Palette knife
- Straight edge
- Side scraper
- Icing bag and adaptor
- Icing tubes - no.1, 2, 3, 13, 43, 44, 50 and 57
- Frill tube - no.060
- Ribbon for board edging

PME Pointers

The depth of the cake can be reached by sandwiching together two shallow cakes, add a layer of marzipan in-between.

PME Pointers

Paddle a small amount of gum tragacanth into the icing before piping the trellis, this makes the icing stronger and less likely to break during handling.

PME Pointers

Coating the board and the cake separately results in a finer finish to the finished cake.

4 Make twelve copies of the trellis patterns and place them on a 6cm(2½in) curve; cover them separately with run-out film. Paddle the icing and add a large pinch of gum tragacanth for strength. With a no.2 icing tube outline the shape, then pipe the two layers of diagonal lines with the same tube. Finish by over piping the outline with a no.3 icing tube.

5 Trace six copies of the numbers and place them on a flat board under run-out film. Outline with a no.1 icing tube. Leave to dry, then paint the outline gold with edible gold powder and alcohol.
Fill in the numbers with a thick consistency of run-sugar and place immediately under a lamp to dry.

3 Place the cake on the sloped board. Check carefully that it is in the centre, then fill in the gap round the base of the cake with full peak icing. Smooth the icing against the side of the cake. This will also stick the cake to the board. Leave to dry.

PME Pointers

Use the minimum amount of tape to fix the film over the patterns, this makes it easier to remove the piping when it is dry.

6 Trace the outline of the top linework and cut out to make a template. Place on top of the cake and use the points of the template to divide the cake into six sections. Mark the divisions on the side of the cake, top and bottom, with a small bulb.

PME Pointers

Heat from a lamp will result in a good shine on the icing and prevents it from sinking.

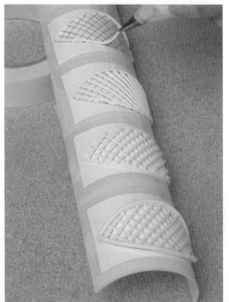

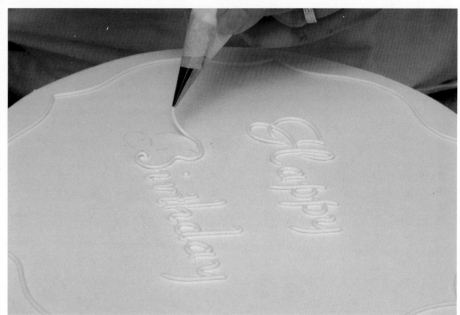

opposite starting bulbs of each pair, this allows for a rose to be inserted later.

12 Pipe an extra scroll with a no.44 tube under the edge of the no.13 scrolls at the top of the cake. Then overpipe all the no.13 scrolls with a no.44 tube.

13 Continue overpiping in the same way using no.43 and no.4 icing tubes.

7 Using a no.2 icing tube pipe a line round the edge of the template.

8 Scribe or trace the lettering on to the cake and pipe again with a no.2 icing tube. When the lettering is dry, paint it gold.

9 Cut out the side template and attach to the side of the cake, with the centre in line with a set of dividing bulbs. Pipe tiny dots round the edge with a no.1 icing tube to mark out the shape. Move the template round the cake until you have completed all six sections.

PME Pointers

A tilting turntable will make the piping on the side so much easier.

PME Pointers

Allow time for the icing to dry a little between the layers of overpiping, or the weight of the sugar will drag the scrolls out of shape.

14 Remove the trellis pieces from the curves. Attach to the side of the cake with royal icing and the point covering the tails of the scrolls. Place a second trellis above it, with the point resting over the top edge of the cake. Pipe two leaves over the centre join.

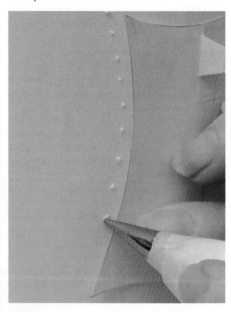

PME Pointers

If you attach the trellis pieces immediately after over piping the scrolls with the no.4 tube, the icing will be soft enough to hold the points in place.

10 Pipe over the tiny dots with an outline of leaves, using a no.50 icing tube to form a frame, then attach the numbers in the centre of each one.

11 Increase the number of divisions to twelve with small bulbs. Place an adaptor and no.13 tube in an icing bag, fill with royal icing. Pipe a series of alternate 'S' scrolls round the top and base of the cake. The twelve divisions determine the length of the scrolls. Leave a small space between the

15 Pipe twelve roses using a no.57 tube, and when dry place them in the centres of the scrolls.

16 Pipe a frill with a no.060 frill tube round the slope of the board, keeping the top of the tube against the top of the slope. Start by touching the surface with the tube, apply pressure and lift the tube away in an upward semicircular motion, before touching back on the surface. This forms a ric-rac effect along the top, and creates the frills along the bottom.

17 Complement the design with a gold ribbon round the edge of the board.

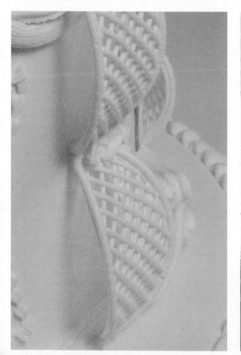

Christmas Santa

This design combines the two mediums of royal icing and flowerpaste to produce an unusual explosion of shape and colour, with Santa playing the central role. The cake and the board are iced separately, because of the different colours.

by
Nadene Hurst

1 Marzipan the cake and place the cake card underneath, then set on a board. Apply three coats of white royal icing, top and sides, finishing with a top coat. Carefully score round the base of the cake with a craft knife to release it from the board, keeping the cake card in place.

PME Pointers

If you remove the cake card from underneath the cake the moisture will make the red colour run into the side coating.

2 Colour approximately 250g (8oz) of icing red, to match the red flowerpaste. Coat the second board, using three coats for a good finish. Leave to dry.

3 Attach the cake to the red board with a small amount of icing underneath, leaving the cake card in position. Carefully fill in any gaps at the base of the cake with white icing smoothing it vertically to the side of the cake.

4 Cut out a 20cm(8in) round template and divide it into twelve sections. Place on top

Checklist • Checklist • Checklist

- Cake - round 20cm(8in)
- Cake card 20cm(8in)
- Cakeboards 2 - round 28cm (11in)
- Marzipan - 750g(1½lb)
- Royal icing - 1kg(2 lb)
- Flowerpaste - red 200g(6oz) green 50g(2oz) white 30g(1oz)
- Colours - red, green, flesh and black

- Dusting powder - yellow, green and red
- Edible varnish
- Rolling pin - small
- Cutting wheel
- Santa cutter
- Three leaf plunger holly cutter - 45mm
- Icing tubes no.2 and 42
- Ribbon for board edging

of the cake and mark each division on the edge.

5 Check the depth of your cake, and cut out a rectangular template 2.5cm(1in) wide and the depth of the cake for the length. Roll out the red flowerpaste very thinly and cut out twelve rectangles; attach these to the side of the cake using the division marks as the centre of each one. Make sure that the strips are level with the edge of the cake, not protruding.

PME Pointers

Use watered down royal icing as glue to prevent the coating from dissolving.

PME Pointers

Roll out enough flowerpaste for only two or three strips at a time, or the paste will begin to dry and crack when you attach it to the cake.

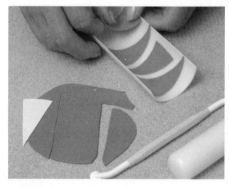

6 Cut out twelve triangles using the template on p112 and dry them inside a 5cm(2in) curve.

7 Roll out some red flowerpaste thinly. Cut out the Santa shape and leave the cutter in position. Insert the impression, and press down firmly. Remove the impression and check before removing the cutter.

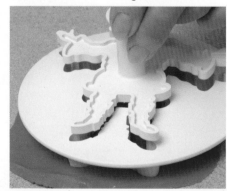

8 Colour a small amount of flesh paste, roll out and impress with the face. Cut out using the cutting wheel or craft knife, and place in position on the Santa. Paint in the eyes and add a ball of paste for the nose.

9 Colour some black paste and cut out boots, belt and gloves, this time use the cutter and the impression; attach them to the figure.

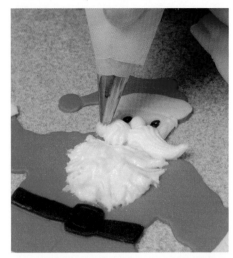

10 From white flowerpaste cut the trimmings for the coat and boots. Use a no.2 icing tip to imprint overlapping circles on each piece to give them a fluffy appearance. Attach each piece to the figure.

11 Use a no.42 icing tip pipe some squiggles of icing over the area of the beard, spread and texture this with a paintbrush. Leave the icing to skin over then pipe two tiny 'S' scrolls for the moustache.

12 Place the impression from the cutter in the centre of the cake and airbrush or petal dust a halo of yellow round the edge. Remove the impression and attach the Santa to the cake.

13 Attach each of the red curves to the edge of the cake lined up with the side strips. Leave them to dry, then fill in any gaps between the two sections with red royal icing. Pipe in a fine line and smooth with the tip of your finger.

14 On the cake side in the middle between the side strips, pipe twelve green lines from top to bottom with a no.2 icing tip.

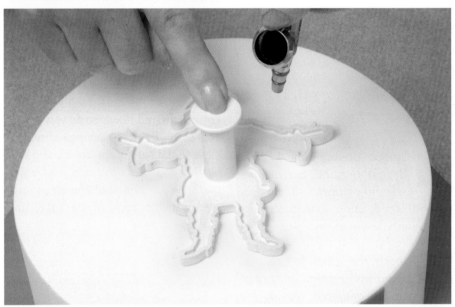

16 For the twelve holly sprigs at the base of the cake, press into the hollows in the foam to create the correct shape. The remaining ones, for the top edge of the cake, should be dried with only a slight indent. When dry, brush the edges with green and red powder and steam.

17 Attach the holly pieces to the base and top of the cake, and pipe three berries in the centre of each one, using a no.2 icing tip and red icing. When the berries are dry, paint them and the leaves with edible varnish.

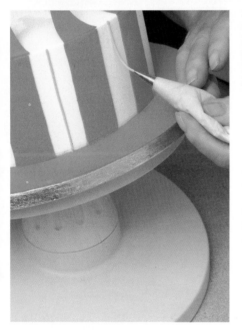

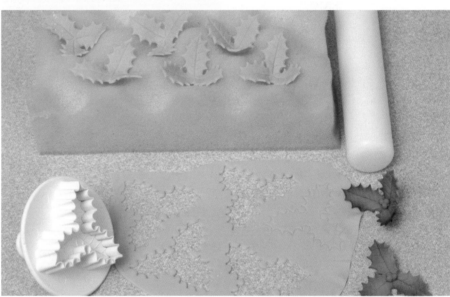

PME Pointers

Tilt the cake on the turntable to make it easier when piping the lines.

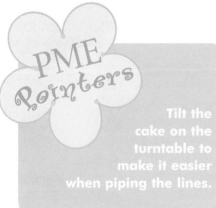

18 Finish off the edge of the board with a matching red ribbon. Happy Christmas!

15 To cut out the holly, roll out the paste thinly and cut, holding the edge of the cutter. Now press down on the plunger for the impression of the veins. You will need twenty four pieces of holly, dried on dimple foam.

Floral Fantasy Wedding Cake

The design of this cake is based on two large daisy shaped cutters creating a fresh, cheerful, appearance. Dependant on cutting out and shaping the daisies, it is simple and quick to execute.

by
Nadene Hurst

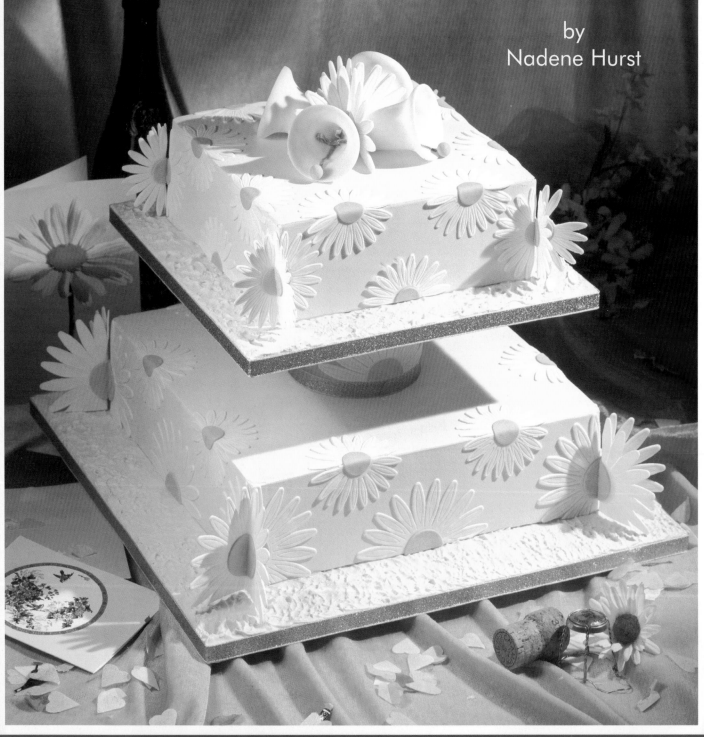

1 Brush the cakes with boiled apricot jam, cover with marzipan, then place on the boards. Apply three coats of royal icing, each coat becoming progressively softer to give a finer finish.

Checklist • Checklist • Checklist

- Cakes - square 20,28cm(8,11in)
- Cakeboards - 28,38cm(11,15in)
- Marzipan - 2.5kg(3 lb)
- Royal icing - lemon - 2kg(4 lb)
- Flowerpaste - white 250g(8oz)
- Sugarpaste - white 100g(4oz)
- Tilting turntable
- Palette knife
- Straight edge
- Veined sunflower/daisy/gerbera plunger cutters - 70,105mm
- Side scraper
- Briar rose cutters - 2,3cm ($^3/_4$,1$^1/_4$in)
- Bell mould - 5.5cm(2$^1/_8$in) diameter
- Ball modelling tool
- Perspex tube - 10cm(4in) diameter - 7.5cm(3in) high
- Ribbon for board edging - gold 0.5,1cm($^1/_4$,$^1/_2$in)

2 When the final coat is dry, use soft peak icing to stipple the board. Do not let the icing creep up the side of the cake, as this will cause problems later.

3 Start with the smallest cake. Roll out some flowerpaste and cut out two of the smaller flowers, impress and eject with the plunger (see next instruction). Cut each in half and attach a piece to each side of a corner of the cake, with edible glue. Repeat for the two remaining corners.

4 To cut out the flowers, first roll out the paste on a thinly greased board, dust the top lightly with cornflour and turn it over. Make sure that the paste moves freely on the surface. Dust again with cornflour before using the flower cutter, this stops the paste sticking to the cutter. Press down the plunger to create veining. Rub the edge of the cutter on the board to ensure a clean cut.

5 For the larger cake use the larger cutter. This will be too tall for the side of the cake and needs to be trimmed at the base to fit.

6 Cut out two more flower shapes of each size, and slice them across the centre. Attach one in the centre at the base of each side of the relevent cake.

10 Attach the folded flowers to the corners of the cake with a line of royal icing.

Top decoration

11 Cut out two of the larger flowers. Cut these across the centre and stick them together, back to back. Cut one section in half again to form two quarter flowers.

7 To complete the flower pattern attach two flowers over the top edge of each side of the cakes. This time use only the smaller size cutter.

8 Mix some darker yellow flowerpaste, roll out and cut centres for the flowers in two sizes, attach with edible glue. Cut the centre in half for the flowers at the base of the cake.

9 Cut out four small and four large flowers, again trimming the larger ones. Attach a deep yellow centre to both sides of the flower, then leave to dry in a 'V' shape. This can be easily made by folding a piece of thin card.

12 When they are dry, assemble into a cross, supporting with foam until firm. Place in the centre of the top cake and attach with piped bulbs round the base.

The bells

13 Mix 100g(4oz) of half and half sugarpaste and flowerpaste. Reserve a small amount for the clappers and divide the rest into four parts. Roll the piece of paste into a smooth ball, then into a short cone. Dust liberally with cornflour and place in the mould.

14 Push the ball tool into the centre of the paste, well down into the mould and twist at the same time. Rub the ball tool round, and up and down the sides to thin the paste and spread it over the sides of the bell.

15 When the centre is big enough continue the moulding with your fingers, smoothing it up to the top rim. Check that it can be easily removed before leaving the bell in the mould until it is firm enough to stand on its own.

18 To make the cake separator attach a 1cm(½in) gold ribbon round the base of the perspex tube using a glue stick. Above the ribbon add three half sections of the larger sized flowers, complete with centres, with edible glue. Finish round the edge of the cake boards with a matching gold ribbon.

16 Tie a small bow in the end of the narrow gold ribbon, trim one tail short and cut off the other tail to the inside depth of the bell. Attach the bow to the inside of the bell as shown, and finish the long tail off with a ball of yellow paste on the rim.

17 Place one bell in each of the spaces round the top ornament, secure with a bulb of royal icing.

Elegant Charm

A combination of piping and run-out skills, together with flawless coating produce a beautifully elegant cake that will please any bride.

by
Nadene Hurst

1 Marzipan the cakes and place on cake cards the same size as the cakes, then stand on some spare cake boards for coating. Leave the marzipan to dry for twenty four hours, then apply three coats of royal icing to the top and sides. Meanwhile coat the three drum boards, in the same way as the top of a cake.

2 Carefully release the cakes from the spare boards, by running the blade of a craft knife round the base, and lift them on to the final coated boards. Fill in the tiny gap round the base with soft peak icing.

3 Draw a series of circles on a spare piece of paper in three different sizes for the three cakes, 3mm($^1/_{16}$in) 5mm($^1/_8$in) and 7mm ($^1/_4$in). Place on a small, flat board, under run-out film. Soften some icing to a thick run-out consistency and pipe bulbs using the circles as an outline guide. You will need at least twelve of each size.

4 Cut out a strip of paper the depth and circumference of each cake. Fold into four sections and trace the side template pattern onto one segment. Keep folded and cut through the four sections to create the template.

Checklist • Checklist • Checklist

- Fruit cakes - round 15,20,25cm(6,8,10in)
- Cakeboards (drums) - round 23,28,36cm(9,11,14in)
- Cake cards - round - the same size as the cakes
- Spare cake boards for initial coating
- Marzipan - 2.5kg(6$^1/_2$lb)
- Royal icing - pale coral pink 3kg(6 lb)
- Gum tragacanth
- Tilting turntable
- Palette knife
- Straight edge
- Side scraper
- Icing tubes No.1, 2, 3,4 and 31R
- Ribbon for board edging

Refer to templates on p116-119

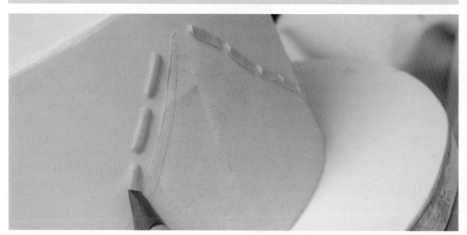

5 Fasten the template round the cake, with full peak royal icing and no.31R tube, pipe short pieces of ribbon (see point six below) following the shape of the template. Remember to leave a space near each point to accommodate the bows.

6 To pipe ribbon pieces keep the end of the icing tube clean to make a good start to each piece. First apply slight pressure and touch the surface of the cake. Then increase the pressure and lift the icing, applying a little tension at the same time, then release the pressure before touching down again to complete the ribbon piece.

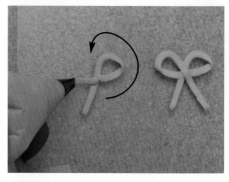

7 Pipe the bows directly onto the cake. Start in the centre and pipe sideways for the width of the loop as shown in the picture. Lift the tube upwards and slightly away from the surface, keep up the pressure, and twist your wrist over to form a loop, then continue downwards to make a tail.

8 For the second loop pipe sideways again, then lift to form a circle before bringing the icing down to form the second tail. Whilst the icing is still wet, attach a bulb to the centre.

9 Use a no.3 icing tube to pipe a line of pearls round the base of the cake.

10 Cut out the templates for the board linework and place in position. Pipe along the inside edge of the template with a no.3 icing tube and leave it to dry. Remove the template and pipe a second line with a no.2 tube, then overpipe the no.3 with the no.2. Overpipe the first line again with a no.1 tube, in a slightly darker colour.

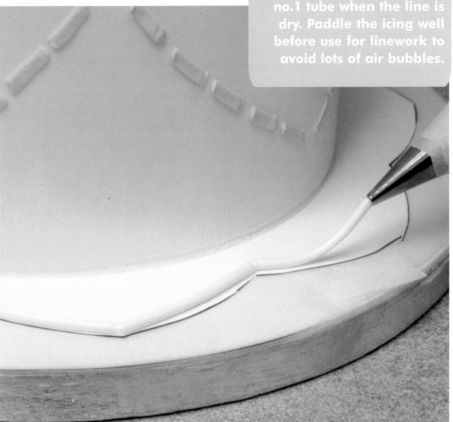

12 Fill in the inside sections with run sugar. Because the outline is such a thick line, only fill in half way up as shown, or your run-outs will be too thick and will probably sink. Place under direct heat to obtain a good shine and dry in a warm place.

13 Overpipe the outline with a no.3 tube, alternating the sequence to cover the joins of

11 Add a small amount of gum tragacanth to the icing to strengthen the icing used for this linework. Place the collar patterns on flat boards under run-out film. For the base and middle size outline with a no.4 icing tube and leave to skin over. Outline the smallest size with a no.3 tube to avoid it looking too heavy.

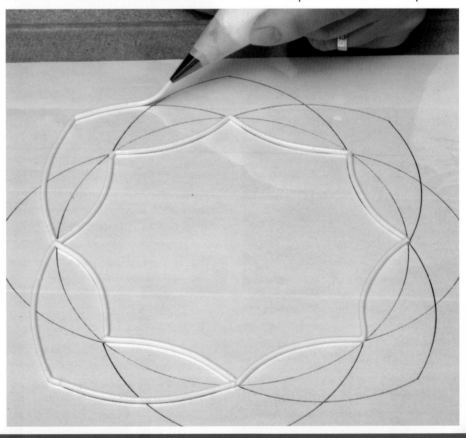

the previous line. Continue overpiping with a no.2 tube, then with a no.1 in a darker shade, again alternating the position of the joins. Leave to dry. Add the bulbs (piped earlier) over the lines at the junctions between the run-out sections. Use softened icing to attach the bulbs, as there is less chance of breaking the linework.

14 Release the collars with a thin, cranked palette knife. Position the top of the cake and the collar at the same level and slide the collar and the run-out film across on to the cake. Carefully pull the run-out film from underneath, whilst holding on to the inside of the collar.

15 Check the position of the collar in relation to the side design, then pipe a line of pearls with a no.3 icing tube underneath, touching both the collar and the top edge of the cake. This will hold it in position.

16 Add suitable co-ordinating flower arrangements to the centre of each tier and attach matching ribbon to the edge of the boards.

Buttercream & Crème Fillings

The decorative use of Buttercream and Crème Fillings gives the opportunity to add wonderful rich flavours to celebration cakes. In many countries especially those that have high humdity these icings are the main decorative medium and in a world of international communication and travel, traditional cakes are being influenced by some of these many and varied styles.

The increased popularity of sponge cakes has opened the way to a wider decorative use of these creams and they are no longer icings used just for gateaux, fairy cakes and fillings.

RECIPES

Traditional Buttercream

This icing can be prepared by hand or by using a food mixer or food processor.

butter 100g (4oz)
icing sugar - sifted 200g (8oz)

1 Place the butter into a bowl and allow it to come to room temperature.

2 Add a small quantity of the icing sugar and beat in.

3 Gradually beat in the remaining icing sugar a little at a time until the icing is pale and fluffy.

4 A small quantity of milk can be added to create a softer texture.

White Decorating and Filling Creme

This white icing has the advantage of taking both colours and flavours extremely well and the texture makes it ideal for piping etc. Prepare by hand or with a food mixer or processor.

white vegetable shortening / fat 200g (8oz)
icing sugar - sifted 500g (1lb)
water or milk 3 tablespoons
glycerin 1 teaspoon
butter flavour 1 teaspoon
vanilla flavour 1 teaspoon
egg white or meringue powder - optional 1 tablespoon (to give added stabilty)

1 Place the white vegetable fat into a bowl and allow it to come to room temperature.

2 Add all of the liquid ingredients including the flavours and beat together until the fat has softened.

3 Gradually add in the dry ingredients and beat until mixed together and the icing is a creamy texture. When the icing is to be used for piping take care not to over beat.

Additional flavours

Lemon - juice and grated zest of 1 Lemon
Coffee - expresso coffee or instant coffee blended with tepid water (1 tablespoon)
Chocolate - cocoa powder blended with tepid water (1 tablespoon)
Liqueurs - fruit & nut liquid flavours (1 teaspoon)

Chocolate Ganache

A luxury chocolate icing that can be poured or beaten into a crème suitable for piping.

whipping cream 400ml (14oz)
chocolate - choice of quality will determine the flavour 450g (1lb)
unsalted butter 125g (4oz)

1 Place the cream into a saucepan and bring to the boil. Remove from the heat.

2 Break up the chocolate and whisk into the cream until smooth.

3 Beat in the butter. The ganache can be used as a poured cake covering whilst still liquid.

4 When used as a filling or in a piping consistency, leave to set overnight and then beat before use.

Coating

1 To coat a cake with buttercream or a crème filling the icing should be a soft consistency and this can be obtained by the addition of either milk or water.

2 Crumb coat (1st coat)
Place the cake onto the cake board. With a palette knife apply the icing generously to the top of the cake, spread evenly and allow the icing to come over the top edge of the cake.

3 Add additional icing to the sides until the cake is completely covered.

4 Using a plain scraper or palette knife, hold it at an angle to the cake sides and skim the icing surface to obtain a smooth coat.

5 To smooth the top, use a clean palette knife and wipe the excess icing towards the centre of the cake. Place the cake to dry allowing the icing to set and crust over.

6 Final coat
Complete the cake covering by adding additional thin layers as required.

The Magic of Steam Trains

For many children and adults a traditional steam train is something very special. This cake has been created using a stencil, a technique that is easy to use with buttercream.

by Pat Trunkfield

1 Coat the cake and board with white buttercream, allow the icing to crust and set.

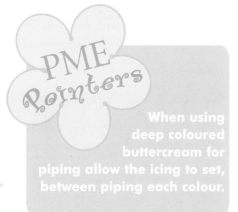
Checklist • Checklist • Checklist

- Round sponge cake 20cm (8in)
- Round cake board 30cm (12in)
- Buttercream 1kg (2lb)
- Food colour - royal blue, yellow, black, brown & green
- Piping bags
- Train stencil
- Icing tubes no's 3, 2, 6, 8 & ST50
- Angled palette knife
- Ribbon for board edging

2 Place the stencil onto the cake with the handle upper most.

3 Use an angled palette knife to spread blue icing evenly over the stencil to fill all of the cut-out shapes. Take care not to move the stencil, use the handle if necessary to hold it in place

4 Wipe the pallete knife across the icing to achieve a smooth finish.

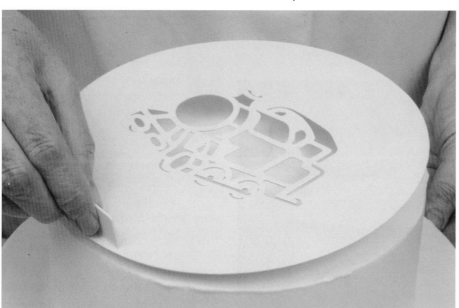

7 Place black icing into a piping bag with a no.3 icing tube. Outline the train and fill in all of the white spaces in between the stencil, this may require increasing the pressure or piping more than one line.

PME Pointers

Use an angled pallete knife to smooth the icing across the stencil. This will keep the fingers above the cake and away from the icing

5 Hold the stencil by the handle and lift it directly upwards to remove it from the cake.

6 Whilst the stencilled train is setting, prepare the coloured icings for the piping,

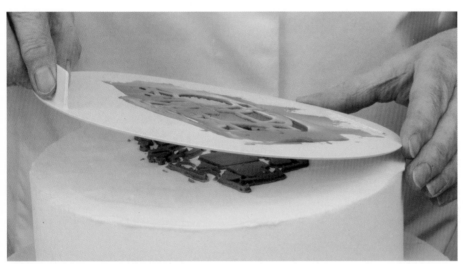

8 Use yellow icing and a no.2 icing tube in the bag to pipe over the black areas to highlight and outline the basic train shape.

9 Lightly blend together a little black icing with a small quantity of white icing and place into a piping bag with a no.6 icing tube. Pipe swirls of icing for the steam and foreground.

10 The trees and fences on the side of the cake are also created using lightly blended

colours of brown and black. Use a piping bag with a no.2 icing tube.

11 Pipe the tree trunks using a random pressure to create texture and interest, beginning at the top of the trunk and working down to the base and roots.

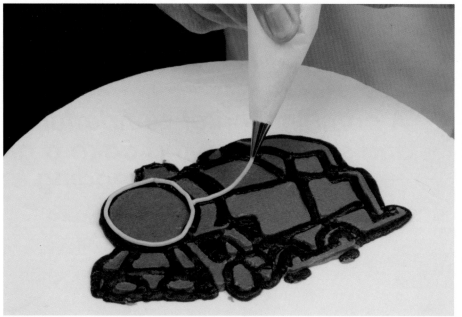

12 Add in the branches. Squeeze firmly to begin with and gradually reduce the pressure.

13 Pipe the fences using the same random pressure technique and piping as many as necessary to fill the spaces between the trees.

14 Once more lightly blend two colours together, this time using green and brown. Place into an icing bag with leaf tube no.ST50.

15 Pipe the leaves using a squeeze and pull technique lifting the icing upwards as it is released.

16 Trim the top edge of the cake with a shell border piped with white icing using a no.8 icing tube.

17 Complete the border by piping a green leaf in between each shell shape.

PME Pointers

This stencilling technique can also be used with royal icing and placed onto a sugarpaste cake.

Summer Wedding

A combination of wonderful flavours, texture and style makes this cake a great choice for a sponge wedding cake.

by
Pat Trunkfield

1 Coat the cakes with yellow buttercream and allow the icing to set and crust. Apply the final coat to the sides using the comb patterned side scraper to create the texture.

2 When the final side coat is set then complete the top covering and allow the buttercream to set and crust. Coat the cake board with white buttercream.

Checklist • Checklist • Checklist

- Sponge cakes - oval 15,20, 25cm(6,8 and10in)
- Cake boards - round 25,30,35cm(10,12 and14in)
- Buttercream 4kg (8lb)
- Food colour - yellow, pink, burgundy & green
- Piping bags
- Adapter or coupler

- Comb patterned side scraper
- Flower nail, extra large
- Icing tubes no's 4,18,20B, 52 & 55
- Cake marker set
- Cutting wheels
- Waxed paper squares
- Flower formers
- Ribbon for board edging

Leave a space the width of a piped line before piping the next basket-patterned line; repeat this pattern until you reach the centre of the cake.

PME Pointers To achieve the best finish to a piped basket weave. Pipe the straight lines just on top of the finish point of the textured basket lines as this will hide any rough edges.

6 Pipe a second straight line using the no.4 icing tube and following the next guideline.

PME Pointers When piping an oval or circular basket weave the length of the horizontal lines will require adjusting as you work towards the centre of the cake.

4 Begin the piping using a no.4 icing tube and yellow buttercream. Pipe a straight line from the centre to the edge of the cake, piping over the embossed guidelines.

5 Using a no.20B icing tube and beginning at the outer edge of the cake pipe a basket patterned line from the adjoining embossed line over the no.4 line and finish at the next embossed guideline.

Basket Weave
3 Divide the top of the cake into an even number of sections using the cake markers and the cutting wheels to create an embossed line.

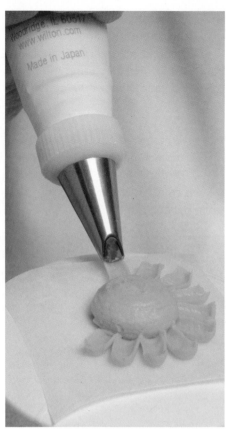

the bulb. Gently continue squeezing as the petal is drawn outwards and lift up slightly at the tip before easing off on the pressure.

11 Continue piping the petals around the bulb to obtain a complete layer.

12 Pipe a second layer of petals, slightly shorter than the first layer and alternating the position with the first layer if possible.

13 Continue piping layers of petals until the bulb is completely hidden. Place to set onto a flower former.

7 Complete the basic basket weave pattern by piping a second row using the no.20B icing tube to fill in the weave spaces left in the previous row. Continue the piped pattern to create the top design.

8 **Chrysanthemums**
Attach a square of waxed paper to the flower nail using a little buttercream to secure in place. Pipe a large round bulb of pink buttercream using a no.18 icing tube.

9 For the petals place the same colour pink buttercream into a bag with the curved petal tube no.55.

10 To pipe the petals squeeze the icing to attach to the base of

PME Pointers

Flowers piped in buttercream can be transferred directly to the cake without waiting for them to dry or set. Slide either a palette knife gently underneath or use flower lifters.

PME Pointers

When colouring the icing green for leaves consider adding a small quantity of the same colour used to create the flowers as this will bring in a similar tonal quality.

14 You will require twelve (12) chrysanthemums in a variety of sizes and shades of pink through to burgundy to decorate the cakes.

Leaves
15 Using green buttercream and a no.52 icing tube, begin the leaves by piping in a gently ruffled effect, taking the tube away from the starting point then moving backwards and returning to the same place.

16 Pipe additional petals to create a complete leaf. Place into the flower former to set. Pipe a selection of different leaf sizes.

17 To complete the cakes pipe a simple rope top and bottom border in yellow buttercream using the plain no.4 icing tube.

18 Gently remove the flowers and leaves from the wax paper and position onto the cakes, securing in place with buttercream.

PME Pointers Although this cake has been created in buttercream, the same design and techniques could be used with royal icing.

Flowers & Foliage

Over the centuries a wide variety of edible pastes have been used to make sugar flowers, but in recent years the demand for detailed realistic sugar flowers has seen the development of specialist pastes often referred to as flower paste, gum paste, floral paste or petal paste. The combination of edible gums and sugars helps to create a decorative medium that can be rolled out finely, helping to create beautiful sugar flowers.

Ready made flower pastes are now easily available from specialist shops and mail order companies, but these recipes may help if you wish to make your own.

Quick Flower Paste

200g (8ozs) sugarpaste

1 teaspoon edible gum - Gum Tragacanth, Gum Tex, or CMC (Tylose)

1 Blend the gum into the sugarpaste, kneading the paste well

2 Wrap the paste in a plastic air tight bag and leave to rest overnight before using.

Flower Paste

500g (1lb) icing sugar

25ml (1oz) cold water

10ml (2 teaspoon) liquid glucose

15ml (½oz) white vegetable fat

10g (1 tablespoon) meringue powder

10g (1 tablespoon) powdered gelatine

15g edible gum - Gum Tragacanth, Gum Tex, CMC (Tylose) or a combination of gums

1 Place the gelatine and water into a small bowl and dissolve the gelatine, either by placing the bowl over a pan of hot water, or carefully using a microwave cooker on low power.

2 Place all of the dry ingredients into a mixing bowl and blend together.

3 Add the liquid glucose and white fat to the dissolved gelatine and warm until all the ingredients are melted and thoroughly mixed together.

4 Pour the combined melted ingredients into the dry ingredients and slowly mix together. Beat well until the mixture becomes whiter in colour.

5 Lightly rub a small amount of white fat over the surface of the paste before placing in an air tight plastic bag to rest overnight. This will allow the gums to develop and create a paste that has a good stretch.

Five Petal Cutter Flowers

by Pat Trunkfield

Roses are probably the most popular sugar flower and traditionally these have always been made using single petal cutters, but in recent years with an ever growing trend to be able to produce flowers simply and quickly other techniques have gradually developed.
The five petal cutters create classic roses as well as being ideal for making many other beautiful flowers e.g. dahlias, blossoms and christmas roses.

Checklist • Checklist • Checklist

- Five petal cutters
- Bone modelling tool
- Bulbulous cone modelling tool
- Sugarcraft knife with ribbon insertion blade
- Rose calyx cutters
- Foam pad
- Flower paste
- Powder food colours
- Floral wires 24gauge
- Gum glue
- Net / tulle
- Ribbon for board edging

4 Place the cutter onto the paste and press down. For the best results slide the cutter backwards and forwards on the work surface. For a full rose cut out 3 five petal shapes using one size of cutter. Cover the spares until required.

PME Pointers

Although three layers of petals will create a classic rose, the number of layers can be changed to obtain a variety of different rose sizes, from buds to full blown.

Roses

To make roses the centres should be firm, prepare them in advance and allow them to dry until the paste is hard.

1 With flowerpaste, mould a basic cone that when laid over a petal shape, fits approximately three quarters of the length and width. The size of the centre cone will vary depending upon the chosen five petal cutter.

2 Make a hook at one end of the wire and dip the hook into gum glue before inserting into the fat part of the cone. Secure firmly in place.

3 Finely roll out the flowerpaste then turn the paste over to ensure that it is moving freely on the work surface.

5 Place one of the cut shapes onto the foam pad and using a dog bone tool positioned half on and half off the edge of the paste, firmly slide the tool around the petals. This will shape and soften the edges. Turn the paste over.

9 **Second layer of petals**
Soften the edges of the petals and turn the paste over, this will help to ensure that the softened petal edges curve outwards.

10 Thread the wire through the centre of the paste and paint a line of gum glue lightly down one side of the first petal. Attach the petal to the centre.

11 Paint the gum glue in the same position on the second petal and tuck the petal slightly inside the first petal. Attach one side of all the remaining petals in the same way.

12 Now go back and secure in turn the unattached side of each petal.

Third layer
13 Soften the edges of the petals, turn the paste over and thread the paste onto the centre.

6 **First layer of petals**
Paint one petal lightly with gum glue. Thread the wire through the centre of the paste and wrap the petal tightly around the top of the cone. Take care to ensure that the tip of the cone is covered and cannot be seen.

7 Attach the remaining petals in the following sequence, no.3, 5, 2 and 4.

8 To ensure that the rose does not become elongated pinch off and remove any excess paste at the base of the cone.

14 Lightly paint the base of each petal and secure in place, stretching the paste if necessary to achieve the correct height. These petals do not require overlapping and additional shaping can also be added to the petals using the finger tips.

Roses grow in many beautiful colours.

Study photographs or the 'real' things to discover a variety of interesting colourways.

PME
Pointers

Consider adding extra interest to the calyx by using the cutting wheels to obtain tiny cuts in the sepal edge.

16 Soften the edges of the petals using the dog bone tool.

17 Paint the calyx with gum glue, thread onto the wire and attach to the base of the rose. Complete the rose by adding a small ball of paste at the base.

15 **Rose calyx**
Choose the appropriate calyx cutter to fit the rose. Roll out the paste finely, cut out the calyx shape and place onto the foam pad.

Dahlia - unwired

3 To shape the petals place the cone tool onto each of the petals in turn, lift up either side of the petal and wrap over the cone tool. Push firmly together to secure the shape. Repeat the same technique with the second layer.

4 Place one layer on top of the other alternating the petals and securing in place with gum glue.

5 To create the flower centre, mould a ball of paste and texture using net or tulle. Secure in place with gum glue.

PME
Pointers

To create two coloured petals as shown in the dahlias, simply roll out small amounts of paste in the chosen colours. Lay one colour paste on top of the other and continue rolling out to the required thickness.

1 Roll out a small quantity of flower paste and cut out 2 five petal shapes.

2 Using the ribbon insertion blade fitted to the sugarcraft knife, make a small cut across the petals at the point where the petals join the centre.

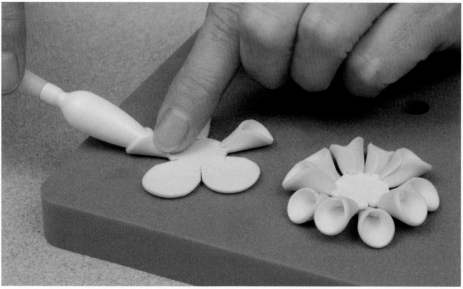

Rose Petal Cutter Flowers

Individual rose petal cutters are the natural choice when making roses, but these traditional petal shapes can also be used for a wide variety of additional flowers, including anemone, blossom and camellia. The individual petals shapes are also ideal to make simple decorations.

by Pat Trunkfield

Open Rose - unwired

1. Roll out finely a small quantity of pale coloured paste.

2. Turn the paste over and ensure that it will move on the work surface.

3. Place the petal cutter onto the paste and press firmly. Slide the cutter backwards and forwards.

4. Lift up the cutter, on most occasions the cut petal shape will remain within the cutter.

5. Check that the cut out petal shape has clean sharp edges and if necessary wipe a thumb or finger over the edges of the paste and cutter to ensure the best finish.

6. Use the bone or ball tool to eject the paste onto the foam pad.

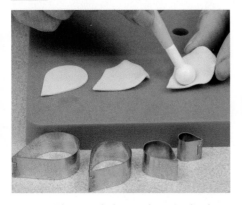

7. Thin and shape the petal edges using the bone tool, keep the modelling tool half on and half off the paste and slide the tool around the edge of the petals.

8. Turn the petal over. With the ball tool, press firmly to cup the petals at the base. Set aside to partially dry.

Make sufficient petals

For the open rose you will require seven large, seven medium and six small petals.

9. Brush with powder food colours as required. For best results brush from the edges of the petal towards the centre with a flat brush.

10. To assemble the flower use either royal icing or softened sugarpaste as a glue.

Checklist • Checklist • Checklist

- ■ Rose flower/petal cutters
- ■ Ball modelling tool
- ■ Bone modelling tool
- ■ Rose calyx cutters
- ■ Cutting wheels
- ■ Foam pad
- ■ Flower paste
- ■ Stamen
- ■ Powder food colours
- ■ Flower wires 24gauge
- ■ Gum glue
- ■ Ribbon for board edging

11. Begin by attaching the larger petals in a ring formation directly onto the cake or plaque. The petals do not need to touch in the centre.

12. Add in the additional petals, gradually working towards the centre and arranging the petals so that they alternate with the previous layer.

13. Complete the flower by inserting coloured stamen in the centre.

Wired Roses

1. Begin by making a centre cone to mould the petals around, prepare this in advance and allow to dry overnight. Mould a small piece of flower paste into a cone shape - the size of the cone will determine the rose size.

2. Bend the end of a wire over to form a small hook. Dip the hook into gum glue and insert into the base of the cone shape. Ensure that it is firmly in place, before placing the cone to dry.

3. Use finely rolled out flower paste to cut out small rose petal shapes. Soften the edges of the petals using the dog bone tool.

4. Paint the first petal with gum glue and wrap around the top of the cone, ensure that the tip of the cone is completely hidden.

5. Paint a small amount of glue at the base of the petal and attach to the flower centre. Place additional petals overlapping each other and ensure that they are wrapped firmly around the centre.

6. The petals are added in layers and the size of the rose will depend upon the number of petals and layers that are added.

Rose Calyx

7. Choose the appropriate calyx cutter to fit the rose. Roll out the paste finely and cut out the calyx shape.

8. Use the cutting wheels to create additional detail to the edges of the petals.

9. Place the calyx onto the foam pad and soften the petal edges using a dog bone tool.

10. Paint the calyx with gum glue and thread onto the wire and attach to the base of the rose.

11. Mould a small ball of paste, thread onto the wire and secure in place to complete the rose.

Foliage

Leaves are the natural accompaniment to flowers and are also wonderful as a decoration in their own right.

by Pat Trunkfield

PME Pointers

When cutting out leaves use pale green or cream coloured paste as this allows a wide choice of colouring and shading.

Checklist • Checklist • Checklist

- rose leaf plunger veiner cutters
- ivy leaf plunger veiner cutters
- holly leaf plunger veiner cutters
- dog bone modelling tool
- foam pad
- flower paste
- floral wires 26 gauge
- powder food colours in shades of green, red and yellow.
- edible glaze

Basic Technique

1 Roll out the paste evenly.

2 Place the cutter onto the paste and cut-out the leaf without pressing the plunger.

3 Press the plunger down to emboss the leaf veins.

4 Lift up the cutter and press the plunger once more to eject the cut out shape.

5 The basic veining and shape of the leaf can be highlighted by brushing with powder food colour before gently curving and shaping as required.

Wired leaves

1 Roll out the paste evenly. It should be thick enough to insert a wire.

2 Cut out, emboss and eject the leaves using the basic technique.

3 Hold the leaf firmly between the thumb and the first finger. Dip the end of the wire into water or gum glue, then insert it into the base of the leaf. Thread the wire approximately halfway into the length of the leaf.

4 Place the leaf onto the foam pad and use a dog bone tool to soften and shape the edges.

Rose leaves – soften the leaves from the back and pinch the tip of the leaf to create a sharper shape.

Holly leaves – soften the leaves from the front; to accentuate and sharpen the needles of the holly, press firmly with the modelling tool in between each point.

Ivy leaves – these are basically a flat leaf and therefore do not require a lot of shaping.

5 Pinch the base of the leaf firmly around the wire and place to dry.

6 The leaves can be coloured by brushing with a variety of powder colours including red for the rose leaves and blue for the holly and ivy.

PME Pointers

After brushing with powdered food colouring highlight the centre veining with a darker colour – eg red, blue or dark brown.

7 To paint the leaves with a variegated pattern, mix paste or powdered colours with clear alcohol and begin painting with pale shades gradually working through to darker colours.

PME Pointers

Consider making simple berries to add interest to both the holly and the ivy leaves

Adding a shine

Steaming – this technique will create a gentle shine and is often referred to as setting the colour. Simply pass the coloured dry leaves through the steam from a kettle, taking care not to soften them with too much moisture. Remember that steam is very hot and should be treated with care.

Glazing – Edible glaze or varnish can be used at full strength to produce a high shine or diluted with clear alcohol to reduce the intensity. To achieve an even coating, place the glaze into a wide top glass jar and dip the leaf into it, remove any excess before placing the leaf to dry.

CYMBIDIUM ORCHID

The cymbidium is a very popular orchid.
The name cymbidium is derived from the Greek
and refers to the boat-like appearance of the lip.

by Ulla Netzband

Column

1. Roll a small ball of paste into a teardrop and insert a 10cm (4in) hooked 26g wire. With a small handle of a paintbrush hollow out the inside and press the tip of the paste over to form a cobra head.

2. Leave the paintbrush handle inside the column then, with tweezers, make a raised vein just inside the outer edges on both sides.

3. Roll a tiny ball of paste and glue it right at the tip of the cobra head. Mark the centre with the wheel and leave to dry.

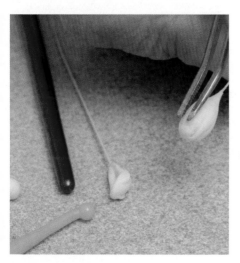

Labellum (throat/lip)

4. Roll out the paste with a centre ridge. Cut out the throat shape.

5. Thin the edges with the bone tool and draw a centre vein with a wheel. Mark a raised vein with tweezers near the narrow end on either side of the centre vein.

6. Frill the outer edges but not too heavily. Add a little glue on both sides of the narrow end and fold this over the column.

Petals and Sepals

7. Roll out the paste with a little bump in the middle. Cut out the shape and elongate all petals and sepals with a bone tool.

PME Pointers

Add interest to your orchid stem by letting each flower face into a different direction.

8. Using a bone tool and starting at the tip roll the dorsal sepal forward. Turn the shape over and roll the other petals and sepals back.

9. Turn the paste over again and thread the column and throat into the bump. Secure with a little rosewater. Tape the wire with nile green tape.

Colouring

10. Dust deep inside the throat with a mixture of primrose and white. Paint dots inside the throat and on the inside of the column by mixing dust with alcohol. Dust the flower with the chosen colour.

Assembly

11. Take a 22gauge wire and form a small bud using tape onto the wire. Add in an orchid with the stem showing. At intervals add in more orchids, always offsetting them.

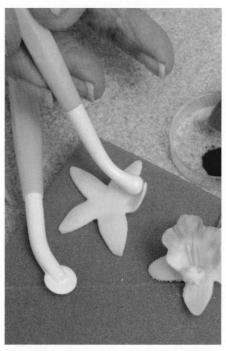

12. Make a second, slightly shorter stem and attach this to the main stem. Make a third much shorter stem and attach to the other two stems.

13. Dust the stem with moss green and a little of the colour used on the labellum. Twist all the stems into an attractive shape. When dry put the stem through the steam of a kettle.

Cattleya Orchid

For many growers cattleyas are the archetypal orchid with their large flamboyant flowers, often with frilled lips and petals. The colours include rich glowing mauves and purples, red and soft pastel pinks.

by Ulla Netzband

1 **Column**
Roll a pea size piece of paste into a carrot shape and insert a 10cm(4in) 24gauge hooked wire.

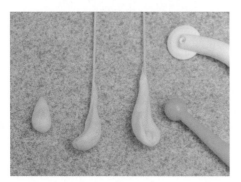

2 With a small paintbrush handle, hollow out the underside. At the broad end of the column, furthest away from the wire, pinch out a little flap on either side of the wire.

3 Draw a line from the wire end on the inside edge on both sides.

4 Roll a tiny ball of paste and with rosewater attach it right at the tip of the column. With angled tweezers divide this into two sections.

5 **Labellum** (throat/lip)
Roll out the paste - not too fine. Cut out the shape.

6 Frill the outer edge heavily. Put a little glue on either side of the narrow end and fold the throat over the column allowing the paste to overlap a little.

7 **Petals**
Roll out the paste and lay a 10cm(4in) 28gauge wire over it. Fold the paste over and roll again. Cut out the shape.

8 Use the frilling tool to thoroughly frill all the edges. Make a second petal reversing the shape.

9 **Sepals**
Roll out the paste and lay a 10cm(4in) 28gauge wire over it. Fold paste over and roll again. Cut out the shape

10 Thin the edges but do not frill the sepals. Make three. The dorsal sepal curves forward and the other two sepals curve back.

11 **Buds**
Tape a whole length of 24gauge wire, cut into five or six sections, add a hook to each one.

PME Pointers

Cattleya orchids look very attractive arranged as a buttonhole or corsage, just add some filler flowers and foliage.

PME Pointers

Assemble flowers before they have dried completely. There is less chance of breakage and it is still possible to re-shape the petals.

12 Roll a small piece of paste into a rounded bud , add a little rosewater to the hook, insert a wire and secure. Use the plain wheel to divide the bud into five sections.

13 **Colouring**
With lemon dusting powder, dust the anther cap and deep inside the throat. Dust petals, sepals and the base of the throat your chosen colour. Consult a book or look at a real orchid for ideas. Dust the buds a mid green colour.

14 When the paste is dry put through the steam of a kettle to set the colour.

Phalaenopsis Orchid

The name means 'resembling a moth' and it is also known as the moth orchid. They are large waxy flat oval-shaped flowers on long stems. The colours vary from white, to pink, purple and yellow.

by Ulla Netzband

1 Labellum (Lip/throat)
Roll out paste with a centre ridge and cut out the shape, insert a 12cm(4.5in) 26gauge wire into the ridge for two thirds of the length.

2 Use fine scissors to cut the unwired piece into a 'V' shape creating two very fine strands. Curl strands inwards with a small bone tool.

3 Cup and slightly vein the two side lobes with the miniature friller. Make a raised vein with tweezers, squeezing either side of the wire between the two side lobes.

4 Make a tiny ball of white paste and set this over the ridged vein in between the side lobes. Split this ball into two sections with cranked tweezers. Before the paste gets too dry curve the labellum forward so that the two curling strands bend inwards.

5 Column
Roll a small piece of white paste into a small teardrop, hollow the underside out with the miniature bone tool creating a little cobra head. Bring the tip to a point and attach the column to the lip.

6 Lateral (wing) petals
Roll out the paste thinly with a thicker point at the base. Cut out the shape and insert a hooked 12cm(4.5in) 28gauge wire into the base.

7 Thin the edges with a ball tool and vein on a suitable veiner. Allow the petals to fall back slightly. Make a second petal reversing the shape for the opposite side.

8 Dorsal and Lateral Sepals
Roll out the paste thinly and leave a ridge where the sepals meet. Insert a 12cm(4.5in) 28gauge wire into the ridge. Thin the edges with a ball tool, vein and set shape over dimpled sponge.

9 Assembly
Place the two petals either side of the column. Add the sepals behind and in between the petals. Thicken the stem with tape.

10 Buds
Tape a whole length of 24gauge wire. Cut into sections and make a hook. Roll a ball of green paste, leaving the tip fairly blunt, put a little rosewater onto the hook and insert the wire. Use a cutting wheel to divide the bud into five sections. Make the buds in different sizes.

11 Leaves
Roll out green paste and lay a 24gauge wire over it. Fold the paste over and roll again. Cut out rounded ovals free-hand. Soften the edges with a ball tool and vein.

12 Colouring
Dust the centre of the throat with a little lemon dust. With a fine paintbrush or cocktail stick paint little dots and lines into the centre of the labellum radiating out. Dust the labellum with a mixture of deep purple and plum, leaving the centre yellow. Dust a little of the deep purple/plum mixture to the base of the wing petals. Dust the buds with foliage and overdust with light green. Dust the leaves with foliage and overdust upperside with forest green. When dry, steam and dip into half glaze.

13 Assembly of stem
Take an 18gauge wire and attach the smallest bud, leaving about 2cm(3/4in) of the stem exposed.

Add more buds at intervals to both sides of the stem, increasing their size. Add the flowers at intervals. Curve the stem.

14 Dust the stem with moss and steam the whole stem.

Sweet Pea

*The name sweet pea is believed to have first
been used by the poet Keats. The most popular
variety is the climbing sweet pea.
They come in a large range of colours.
The meaning of sweet pea is blissful pleasure.*

by Ulla Netzband

1 Keel

Make an open hook on a 10cm (4in) 26gauge wire. Roll a small piece of paste into a pasty shape and attach to the wire. With finger and thumb make a fine ridge on the upper part and let the tip fall back. You should now have a thicker centre and a fine ridge. Open the fine ridge with a scalpel.

2 Wing and standard petal

Roll out some paste leaving a centre ridge for about one third of the way up the petal. Cut out the shape and insert a 10cm(4in) 28gauge wire into the ridge.

3

Frill the edge following the shape of the petal. Soften all the edges with a bone tool. With finger and thumb reinforce the centre vein. Point the tip of standard petals and bend back slightly.

Checklist • Checklist • Checklist

- ◼ Rose petal cutters
- ◼ Sweet pea cutters
- ◼ Plain cutting wheel
- ◼ Veiner tool
- ◼ Bone tool
- ◼ Miniature frilling tool

- ◼ Flower paste - white, pale green
- ◼ Wires - white 26,28,33,35 gauge
- ◼ Dusting powder: colours to choice
- ◼ Rosewater
- ◼ Florist tape - nile green

6 Buds

Make a small keel on a 10cm(4in) 26gauge wire and shape as for flower.

9 Leaves

Cut out some wired oval shapes freehand. Thin the edges with a ball tool and vein with the veiner tool following the shape of the leaf.

10 Colouring

Dust the keel and calyx with spring green. Dust the petals with the chosen colour starting at the edge and bringing the colour in. Dust the upper leaves with forest green and overdust both sides with spring green.

PME Pointers

Wiring wing petals and standard petals separately makes for a stronger flower and gives more movement to it.

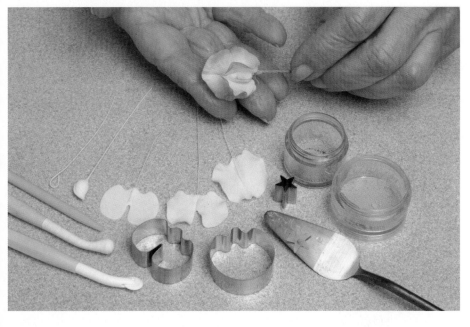

4 Assembly

Tape the keel to the wing petal with third width nile green tape. The tip of the keel should protrude through the centre of the wing petal. Next, tape on a standard petal.

5 Calyx

Make a tiny mexican hat and cut out the shape with the little star cutter. Elongate each sepal with the bone tool. Hollow out the centre with a cocktail stick. Attach two sepals behind the flower either side of the centre seam, the other three to the front and side of the flower curling it downwards.

7

Roll out paste and cut out a shape with a rose petal cutter and cut a 'V' from the rounded end of the cutter at the top of the petal. Frill and vein as for the flower and attach this behind the keel.

8

Roll out paste and cut another rose petal the same size and frill and vein as before and attach behind the standard petal. Pinch the centre seam of this petal and let it fall slightly away from the wing petal. Make a calyx as before.

The tendrils grow from the axis of the leaves. Do not attach them to the flower stem.

11 Tendrils

Tape a whole length of 35gauge wire with quarter width nile green tape. Cut the wire into sections and curl over a paintbrush. The tendrils grow from the axis of the leaves.

12 Assembly

Take a couple of buds with their stem showing and attach these to a 24gauge wire in uneven length. Add more buds and flowers, in groups of two or three, to the stem. Make a few stems. Strengthen the wire when necessary.

13

Make some leaf stems. Take a 24gauge wire and attach a pair of small leaves with tendrils. Tape more leaves on, always in pairs, increasing their size as you run down the stem. Combine flower and leaf stems.

DAISY

Countless writers from Chaucer onwards have written in praise of the humble daisy. The flower stalk is leafless. Each solitary flower-head has a yellow disc surrounded by a ring of white rays.

by Ulla Netzband

1 Flower

Make a short mexican hat using green paste. Cut out the shape with the smaller daisy cutter. Insert a taped hooked 10cm(4in) 26gauge wire and leave to dry.

2

Roll out white paste and cut two shapes with the larger cutter. Using the plain wheel, cut each petal into half and separate them. Use the veiner to indent each petal in the centre.

3

Place one shape onto a sponge and glue the centre. Position the second shape on top interlocking them as much as possible. With a bone tool indent the centre.

8 Larger bud

Tape and hook a 10cm(4in) 26gauge wire. Roll a small ball of white paste. Cut a shape using the smaller daisy cutter. Split each petal into half. Thread the shape onto the wire. Close the petals around the ball at the tip.

9 Leaves

Cut out wired shapes using two of the rose cutters. Thin the edges with a ball tool. Pull out the edges with a modelling tool. The veins can be marked with the wheel. These radiate out from the base. Look at a book or a real leaf for construction.

4

Glue the prepared calyx and position the daisy shapes onto the calyx, again indenting the petals a little more with a bone tool.

5

When it is semi-dry, roll a small ball of yellow paste and mark it with a piece of tulle. Paint the upper side of this little shape with strong glue and sprinkle a mixture of semolina and lemon dust on to it.

6

Put a little strong glue onto the centre of the petals, position the centre in the middle and leave to dry.

7 Small buds

Tape and hook a 10cm (4in) 26gauge wire. Roll a small piece of white paste into a teardrop and attach to the wire. Draw eight lines on the bud using a wheel.

10 Colouring

Dust the very tips of the daisy with a little pink. Dust the leaves with a mid green dust.

11 Assembly into a pot

Hold all the flowers and buds together and bind with tape at the base of the stems.

12

The leaves form a rosette at the base of the plant. Tape these in. Insert the arrangement into a little pot.

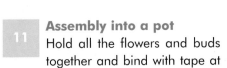

PME Pointers

When making flowers a detailed picture or the 'real thing' helps to make assembly of the flower more acccurate

PME Pointers

Gather all your material together onto foam, ready for assembly.

GERBERA

Gerbera is a genus comprising about forty species. A massive array of colours are available; white, pink, red, yellow, orange and purple. Some gerbera centres are brown, others may be green.

by Ulla Netzband

1. Centre
Make a ski-stick on an 18gauge wire. Roll a ball of paste and press this into the centre of the gerbera cutter. Dip the ski-stick into strong glue, insert it into the ball of paste and leave to dry.

2.
Mix semolina and the chosen dust colour, paint the upperside of the paste with strong glue, dip into the mixture and leave to dry.

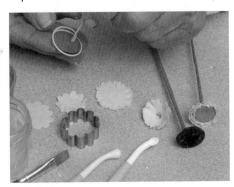

3.
Roll out paste and cut out three rounds with the carnation cutter. Make three to four little cuts into each petal. Separate the notches and flute the outside edges with the modelling tool. With a little rosewater attach these layers quite firmly beneath the centre, letting the frilled edges stand proud.

PME Pointers
Put a little grease on the edges of the cutter to get a sharper cut.

4. Petals
Roll out the paste, not too thinly, cut out a petal shape and turn cutter over with paste still attached. Run your thumb over the entire surface to get a clean cut and good veining.

5.
Push paste out onto a soft pad. With a ball tool thin the edges. Turn the shape over, run the ball tool over each petal from the tip towards the centre to curl each petal outward. Dust this layer with the chosen colour.

6.
Moisten underneath the centre with rosewater and attach the petal securely behind it. Hang upside down.

7.
Make one more round of petals. Again dust the layer as before, attach it to the previous layer making sure to place the petals in between the petals of the previous layer. Hang upside down until semi dry. Make a former with foil, insert the flower and leave to dry.

8. Calyx
Roll a piece of green paste into a small oval shape and attach behind the flower with a little rosewater. Roll out green paste and cut out two daisy shapes and divide each petal into two.

9.
Stretch the petals with a bone tool. Put a little rosewater onto the centre of one of the shapes, place the other one on top making sure to interlock the sepals.

10.
Place onto a sponge and indent the centre with a ball tool.

11.
Brush a little rosewater behind the flower. Thread the calyx on.

12.
Roll out some green paste and cut a small daisy shape. Separate the petals again and using a bone tool stretch them.

13.
Thread onto the previous two, again interlocking. Leave to dry.

14. Colouring
Dust the petals lightly with the chosen colour. Then dust the calyx with moss green.

15. Assembly
Gerberas grow on single stems. The flower stem is fairly thick. Either tape the stem with a few layers of full width tape, or thicken the stem with strips of kitchen roll, finally add a layer of tape. Bend the stem a little forward. Dust the stem with moss and a little of the colour used for the petals.

SUNFLOWER
(Helianthus)

The sunflower was once an emblem of the Sun God of the Incas. In colour it spans the whole range of browns and yellows, to bright yellow with dark brown centres.

by Ulla Netzband

1 Centre

Make a ski hook on an 18gauge wire. Take a ball of brown paste and press this into the centre of the large sunflower cutter. Dip the ski hook into strong sugar glue and press it into the paste. Leave it overnight to dry.

2 Make a mixture of couscous or semolina and brown petal dust. Paint the upper surface of the centre with strong sugar glue and press into the couscous mixture. Leave to dry. Strengthen the stem with an extra 18gauge wire.

3 Dust a little black into the centre and dust the outer edges with egg yellow dust.

4 Petals

Roll out yellow paste and cut a petal shape. Turn the cutter, with the paste still inside, over and run your thumb over each petal to get a clean cut and good veining.

5 Place the cutter and paste onto a pad, press the plunger to release the paste. Turn the petals over and with a bone tool curl each petal back from the tip to the centre.

6 Dust this layer on both sides with a mixture of lemon and egg yellow dust.

PME Pointers

Steam the dried centre before attaching the petals. This will avoid staining the petals.

7 Brush underneath the centre with rosewater and attach the petals securely behind it. Hang upside down. Repeat this making two more layers. Ensure that each layer of petals are interlocked. Make a former with foil and allow the flower to dry.

8 Calyx

Roll out green paste and cut two rose petals from the same size cutter. Elongate each petal and bring it to a point.

9 With a modelling tool make a centre vein and pinch the tips together. Interlock both sepals and attach behind the flower with a little rosewater.

10 Roll out green paste and cut a rose petal with the smaller cutter. Treat as above and attach it behind the previous two, again interlocking it. Dust the calyx with moss green. Thicken the stem by taping with extra layers of full width nile green tape.

PME Pointers

If the flowers are to be arranged upright strengthen the stem with two extra 18gauge wires before attaching the calyx.

11 Assembly

Take one flowerhead and quite closely behind, attach a small leaf. Run the tape down for a short distance and add another small leaf. Add leaves as needed, increasing them in size, remembering that the leaves are off-set. Treat the bud in the same way.

Bend the stem slightly forward.

FUCHSIA

These dainty pendant flowers, native to Central and South America, come in a fascinating range of colours and colour combinations, from brilliant reds and purples to delicate misty pastels. The flowers, borne either singly or in terminal clusters, are single, semi-double or double. As the fuchsia is a very showy, vividly coloured flower, it is best displayed by itself.

by Ulla Netzband

1 Centre

Take nine full length stamen, place them together unevenly leaving one extra long to form the pistil and tape them onto a 10cm(4in) 26gauge wire. Attach a small piece of paste to the base of the stamens and leave to dry.

2 Skirt

Roll out the paste and cut out four rose petals. Ball tool the edges to thin. Put a little glue at the base and a little way up the right-hand side of each petal. Overlap each petal by about two-thirds.

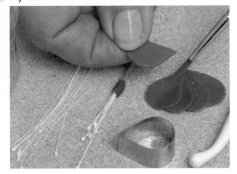

3

Add a little more glue to the first petal and wrap the petals around the centre, ensure that all the petals are even nearest to the tip. Hang upside down.

NOTE: To make a semi-double fuchsia cut out 4 or 5 more petals. Ball tool the edges to thin, cup the centres with a ball tool and pinch the base of each petal together. Attach these in between the first layer. To make a double fuchsia repeat the second layer Use a cocktail stick and roll one edge of each petal over the stick to allow the side to furl back a little.

4 Sepals

Make a mexican hat and cut out a shape using the sepal cutter. Thin the edges with a ball tool and draw a centre vein with a wheel. Use a bone tool to curl the sepals back from the tip towards the centre.

5

Use a cocktail stick to open up the centre. Glue the base of the skirt and thread it into the centre of the sepals. Roll the paste down the wire to form the pedicel. Roll a small ball of green paste into an oval shape and push onto the wire allowing it to merge with the pedicel. This represents the ovary.

Checklist • Checklist • Checklist

- Fuchsia sepal cutter
- Single petal rose cutter
- Rose leaf cutters
- Plain wheel
- Veiner
- Bone and ball tool
- Rose leaf veiner
- Seed-head or round white stamen
- Flowerpaste: colour of choice, green
- Wires-white: 22,26,28 gauge
- Dusting powder: foliage, moss, red, colours of choice
- Fine paintbrush
- Rose water
- Alcohol
- Florist tape-nile green

6

Make fine lines down the pedicel and deeper lines in between each sepal.

7 Buds

Tape a 28gauge wire with nile green tape, cut into sections, add a hook. Roll a ball of paste into a fat teardrop with a fine point at the tip and insert the wire. Roll the paste down the wire, the same length as for the flower. Add an ovary as before.

8

Divide the bud into three parts with a wheel and make fine lines in between using the wheel.

9 Leaves

Cut out a wired shape with a rolled leaf cutter. Thin the edges with a ball tool and vein with the rose leaf veiner. Leave to dry.

PME Pointers

Arrange these showy flowers so they hang gracefully in their natural style

10 Colouring

Dust the stamen the same colour as the sepals. Dust the skirt the chosen colour. Dust the ovary green and brush full strength glaze onto the ovary. Dust the buds the same colour as the sepals. Dust the leaves with foliage and then moss.

11 Assembly

Take a 22gauge wire and attach a couple of buds at uneven lengths leaving about 2cm (³/₄in) of the stem showing.

12

Attach a pair of leaves with a little stem showing. Join in more flowers and buds singly or in clusters. Dust the stem with moss and overdust with a little red dust. Leave to dry, then steam the whole stem.

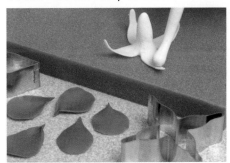

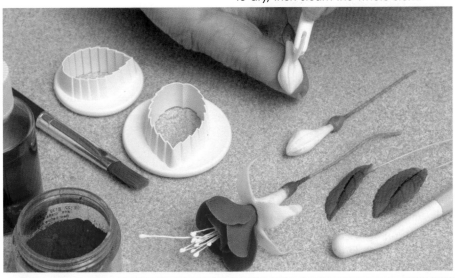

White Bryony

6 **Tendrils** - Tape a 33gauge wire with quarter width nile green tape. Dust with moss green and cut the wire into different lengths. Roll the wire over a paintbrush to curl.

7 **Colouring** - Dust the flower with a very pale mixture of pale green and white. Mix alcohol with moss dust and paint some fine lines onto each petal on both sides. Dust the calyx with moss green and dust the buds similarly.

8 Dust the berries in various colours using green, lemon tangerine and red. Dip in full strength confectioners' glaze. Dust the upper side of the leaves with foliage. Dust both sides with moss green. Glaze in quarter glaze.

1 **Centre** - Fold one stamen in half and glue the cotton strands together with the heads even. Make five of these and leave to dry. Glue the stamen heads and dip into semolina mixed with moss dust. When dry, tape all five onto a 6cm(2.5in) long 28gauge wire. Buds do not need stamen, just a small ball of paste and petals tightly furled.

2 **Flower** - Roll out white paste thinly leaving a tiny bump in the centre. Cut out and elongate each petal then thin the edges with a bone tool. Using a cutting wheel draw a centre vein on each petal. Attach the flower to the centre with the bump underneath, secure with a little rosewater. Hang upside down until semi-dry.

3 **Calyx** - Make a small mexican hat and roll out the paste. Cut out the shape with the star cutter. Attach behind the flower. Position the sepals in between the petals.

4 **Berries** - Tape a 30gauge wire and cut into short sections. Hook the wire. Roll a small ball of paste and attach to the wire with rosewater. Cut small pieces of black thread and insert into the tip of the berries leaving the cotton just protruding. Leave to dry.

5 **Leaves** - Place wire between two layers of rolled paste, cut out the leaves and shape.

9 **Assembly** - The tendrils, berries and flower clusters shoot from the junction of the leaf and main stem. The flowers grow on a short stem. The leaves are single and alternate. Tape together as appropriate.

Wood Anemone

Checklist • Checklist

- Wood anemone cutter
- Bone tool
- Cutting wheel
- Corn veiner
- Stamen - very fine yellow
- Flower paste - white and pale green
- Wires-white 26,28,33,35 gauge
- Dusting powder: lemon, moss, foliage, forest, red, rose
- Florist tape - brown $\frac{1}{3}$ width
- Strong sugar glue
- Rosewater

5 **Open bud** - Prepare as previously. Cut out a few petals. Glue and attach these around the ball.

6 **Leaves** - Use 33gauge wire and green paste to create leaf segments, tape the largest leaf with two smaller either side.

7 **Colouring** - Dust flower centres with moss and the stamen heads with lemon. Dust the base of flowers and buds with rose or violet. Dust the upper surface of the leaves with forest and a little red on the edges, then both sides with foliage. Steam the flowers and leaves.

1 **Centre** - Double over 30 fine stamen and attach around a 26gauge wire, leave the stamen-heads 5mm(¼in) above the wire. Tape securely. Attach a tiny ball of green paste centrally, indent with little pinholes.

3 Cup petals in the centre with a small bone tool. Make six petals per flower. Attach to the centre with three inner petals then three petals between and behind.

4 **Closed bud** - Tape 26gauge wire and add a hook. Roll a small ball of white paste, attach and divide into three sections with a cutting wheel.

2 **Flower** - Roll out some white paste leaving a bump at the base. Cut out then insert a hooked 28gauge white wire into the thicker base. Thin edges and vein in a corn veiner.

8 **Assembly** - Two-thirds of the way up each slender flower stem add a ring of three leaves. Slightly bend the flowerhead forward.

Meadow Cranesbill

1 Centre Stigma - Divide the tip of a strong stamen cotton into 5 sections with sharp scissors. Bend the cut sections over to create a little star.

2 Stamen - Paint both ends of 5 fine stamen heads with a mixture of aubergine and alcohol. Cut into half. Dust the stigma with plum and the stamen threads with pale green.

3 Assembly - Attach the stamen around the stigma to a 28gauge wire with tape ensuring that the stigma is higher than the stamen.

4 Flower - Roll paste finely with a little bump in the centre. Cut out. Turn the paste over, on a mat, thin the edges. Slightly elongate each petal. Vein each petal with a wheel following the shape of the petal then cup each petal on a soft sponge. Indent the centre with a bone tool. Thread onto the centre with a little rosewater, with the bump underneath. Secure firmly. Hang upside down until semi dry.

5 Calyx - Cut a calyx from green paste, thin the edges and make a centre vein on each sepal with a cutting wheel. Attach the calyx behind the flower in between the petals.

6 Large bud - Hook a taped 26gauge wire and add a small ball of paste. Add a cut flower wrapping it around the ball. Attach a calyx. **Small bud** - Roll a small oval shape of paste and attach to a hooked, taped wire. Divide the small bud into five sections with a cutting wheel.

7 Cranesbill (seed pod) - Make a stigma as above, attach to a 28gauge wire. Roll a small ball of white paste onto the wire, tapering it very finely towards the stigma leaving about 5mm($^1/_4$in) of the stigma exposed. Make a calyx and attach.

8 Leaves - Wire the paste and cut out a leaf, thin the edges and vein with a cutting wheel.

9 Colouring - Dust the flower with a mix of plum and a little white. Dust the calyx with moss green and a little plum. Dust the large bud as the flower and the small bud with moss green. Dust the stigma of the seed pod with plum and the rest with plum and moss. Dust the calyx with moss and a little plum. Dust the edges of the leaves with plum and the front of the leaves with forest green. Dust both sides with foliage green. Glaze in quarter glaze when the leaf has dried.

10 Assembly - Tape several flowers, buds and seedpods together in uneven length. Add two leaves opposite each other at the base of each cluster. Join together a few stems adding in some leaves.

Lesser Periwinkle *Vinca Minor*

Checklist • Checklist

- Periwinkle cutters
- 5 star tool
- Cone tool
- Bone tool
- Cutting wheel
- Rose leaf veiners
- White wires-22,26,28gauge
- Flowerpaste: white, yellow, and pale green
- Dusting powder: light green, dark green, cornflower blue, fuchsia, lavender
- Rosewater
- Florist tape-nile green third width

throat. Dust from the edges towards the centre of the flower, back and front. Dust the small ball in the centre with light green. Dust the calyx pale green.

1 **Flower** - Form a mexican hat and roll out the paste very finely. Cut with a periwinkle cutter. Soften the edges and slightly cup each petal with a small ball tool. Indent into the centre with the five-star tool.

2 Pull a taped and hooked 26gauge wire through the centre and roll the paste down to cover the wire. If necessary open the throat with the cone tool.
Give petals some movement then leave them to dry. Drop a small ball of white paste into the centre and mark it with a cocktail stick.

3 **Buds** - Attach an oval piece of paste to a hooked, taped 26gauge wire, taper it to a

point at the tip. Mark five deep ridges using the cutting wheel. With finger and thumb pull each section out until the paste is very fine. Spiral the bud around and dust as the flower.

4 **Calyx** - Roll out paste and cut a narrow rectangle, long enough to fit around the base of the flower or bud. Cut five 'V's and wrap it around the base

5 **Leaves** - Create a wired leaf with the oval cutter and vein.

6 **Colouring** - Mix blue, fuchsia and lavender, push a tiny bit of cotton wool down the flower

7 Dust the upper centre of the leaves light green and the outer edges on the upper side with dark green leaving the centre paler. Dust the underneath with moss.

8 **Assembly** - With a taped 24gauge wire add a bud, then a pair of leaves below.
Tape down 1cm(³/₈in) and add a larger bud with a slighter larger set of leaves. Then introduce a flower with another pair of larger leaves.

9 Make a few stems and bind these together, adding a pair of large leaves at the junction of each stem. Dust the stem with a little moss and overdust a little with the blue, fuchsia and lavender mixture. When dry put the stems through the steam of a kettle.

People Moulds

The people moulds will help to produce well proportioned figures. In the set there are moulds for an adult man, adult woman and two sizes for children that can also be adapted to produce smaller adults.

Various craft pastes edible and non-edible are suitable for the moulds. A modelling paste suitable for sugarcraft is given here and many commercial food grade pastes work well. Always wash the moulds when changing crafts.

by Ann Grimshaw

Modelling paste

Icing sugar - 500g(1lb)
Tylo powder 1 level teaspoon
Gum Tragacanth 1 level teaspoon
Powdered Gelatine 15g(1/2oz)
Water 50ml
Liquid Glucose 1 tablespoon
White fat 3 level teaspoons

Soak the gelatine in the water until soft, then dissolve over hot water or in the microwave (do not allow gelatine to boil). Add the liquid glucose and white fat, stir well and set aside to cool slightly.

Sieve the icing sugar with Tylo powder and Gum tragacanth.

Make a well in the centre of the icing sugar mix and add the gelatine mixture. Mix to a firm paste.

Turn the paste out onto a board and knead well. If the paste is sticky knead in some cornflour and extra icing sugar, if too dry add a little white fat.

Wrap the paste in several layers of cling film and store in an airtight container. Leave to mature overnight. Re-knead each portion before use.

Before work commences, decide on the position of the model so the limbs and torso can be arranged appropriately to dry. Adjust the paste to required skin tone.

1 Oil the surface of the mould lightly with a paintbrush. Avoid solid fat or cornflour as these may mask the fine detail of the mould.

2 **Head and torso**
Press a small piece of paste firmly into the face area of the mould so that it comes up to the sides of the mould.

3 Fill in behind with more paste to slightly overfill the remainder of the front mould. Also slightly overfill the back part of the mould then moisten both edges and press the two halves of the mould together.

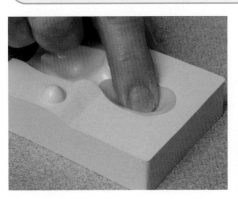

4 Press firmly to squeeze out excess paste then trim away any surplus.

5 Hold the bottom of the mould and the paste firmly and remove the top mould to check the features are correct.

6 Carefully remove the seam of paste around the figure join with a sugarcraft knife.

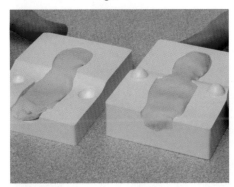

7 Gently remove the figure from the mould, supporting the head and neck trim away any remaining seam before smoothing the join with a modelling tool.

8 Manipulate the figure into the desired posture before inserting a cocktail stick from the base leaving the bottom end of the stick protruding.

9 A short wire can be inserted across the shoulders with ends protruding slightly to support the arms. Any facial adjustments should be done at this stage.

10 **The arms**
Make the arms individually to allow shaping before the paste sets. Lightly oil the mould and slightly overfill the indent, press on the other part of the mould firmly and then remove it. Trim away the seam with particular attention to the hand.

11 Remove the arm from the mould and work on the hand with a small sharp pair of scissors. If required separate the fingers and mark the nails and joints. If the arm is to be bent, remove a 'V' shape from the elbow and secure the bend with edible glue. Make the second arm using the other indent on the mould. Press each arm onto the wires protruding from the torso to create location points for the final assembly. Shape the arms then remove them and support with foam sponge until dry.

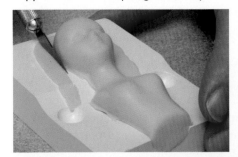

Legs are not always visible so a time saving support may be used e.g. cone shape beneath a long skirt.

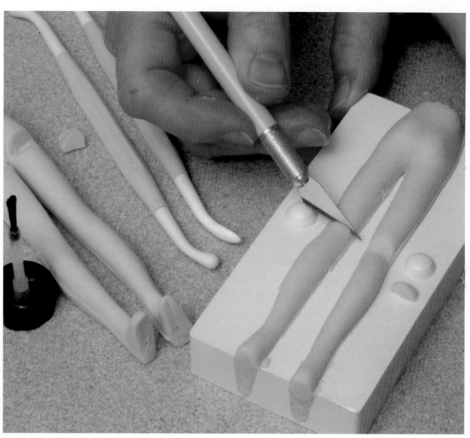

12 The legs

Oil the mould and insert a shaped piece to overfill the space. Press the two halves firmly together. Level the base of the feet by removing any excess paste. Remove the front half of the leg and trim the seams as previously described.

13 If the legs are to stand, strengthen them with wire inserts before removing the legs from the mould. Make an 'L' shaped wire just a little longer than the leg with the angled piece about half the length of the foot. Push this into the leg with the angle pressed into the base of the foot.

14 At this stage press the torso and leg sections together to make indents that will create the location points when the whole is assembled. Adjust the waist if required and bend the legs to the appropriate shape (note point15 below). Remove the legs and lay them down for twentyfour hours to dry, propped in position with scraps of foam sponge.

15 To bend the legs or create a sitting figure, remove a 'V' shape from the back of the knee. Also for a sitting figure remove a further 'V' at the top front of the leg

where it joins the body section. Use short lengths of wire to support bent legs, a full length of wire may break out of the paste as it is shaped.

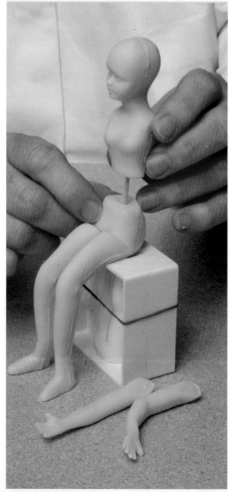

16 To complete the model
Features

Add ears by applying a small tear shape piece of paste to the side seam between the top of the eye and the bottom of the nose. Flatten the forward edge into the side of the face and lift the back edge slightly to stand away from the head. Add further details with a modelling tool and small amounts of extra paste. Check the seams and smooth with an emery board or fill gaps with skin tone royal icing.

17 Face

Apply pale tones gradually and build up the detail of the complexion for a natural effect. Combine white and flesh tone powder colours to brush onto the face for a foundation (for male models use a slightly darker shade). Add a powder blusher sparingly to cheeks.

18 Eyes and mouth

The eyes are very important in creating the overall impression on the face. Decide in which direction the eyes will look. The position of the iris and the amount showing will vary - look at magazine photos for guidelines.

Mark a line across the eye socket where the eyelid will be - there will be very little showing if the model is looking straight ahead but more if the eyes are downcast. Paint the area below the lid white and allow to dry. Mark the position of the pupil, then with eye colour paint in the iris. Darken the pupil and with a craft knife lift a tiny spot to make a highlight. Paint very thin pale lines for eyelashes and eyebrows. Paint the lips - not too brightly - with thinned down paste colour.

19 Hair

Paint a light coloured line to define the shape of the hairstyle around the face. Create the base of the hairstyle by piping with royal icing and a no.2 tube. Add the surface detail with a finer tube and a paintbrush. Hair to stand away from the face can be made with a paste base then coated with royal icing.

20 Assembly and clothing

Roll all paste for clothing as finely as possible. In general a mixture of four parts sugarpaste to one part flowerpaste drapes and models well, although a higher proportion of flowerpaste should be used where elements stand away from the body.

When all the body parts are dry they can be dressed and assembled. First dress the lower limbs taking the seams into the waist. Dress the torso making the seam lines where they would naturally occur and add the torso to the lower body using the location points made earlier. Attach the pieces together with either royal icing or softened modelling paste. Dress the arms with a seam allowance curved around the top of the arm to create a neat seam line at the shoulder. Attach the arms and support them in position with foam sponge until secure.

Assemble the models either singly or in a group onto a plaque or cake drum ensuring that the arrangement is stable. Add extra props or detail to strengthen and enhance the display and to make it more secure for transportation.

PME Pointers

The body parts will be easier to assemble if they are completely dry

The wedding group

The bride's dress has embroidered detail added with no.0 tube. The bridesmaid's dress fabric was initially embossed with the small plunger cutter before assembly then the detail painted onto the garment.

Leaves for the flower arrangements are made from the daisy/marguerite plunger cutter; the petals are separate and veined with a craft knife. The roses for the bride and her attendant have been created from the blossom plunger cutters using a stamen for the centre.

The clematis flowers at the base of the display are cut from the large plunger cutter and the leaves from the middle heart plunger cutter.

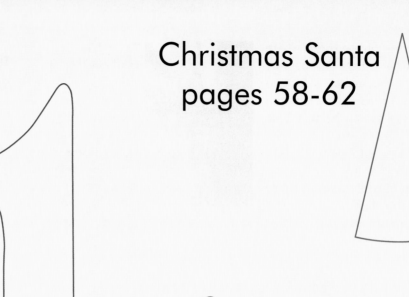

Christmas Santa
pages 58-62

Today

Loveable Teddies
pages 6-9

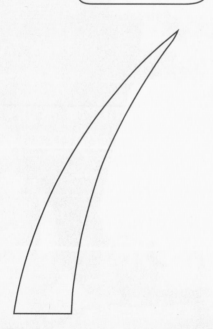

Outside Ribbon Pattern

Inside Ribbon Pattern

Top Pattern and Words

Happy Birthday

Side Template

Trellis Pieces

Pillar

Pillar

Pillar

3rd Tier

Top Tier

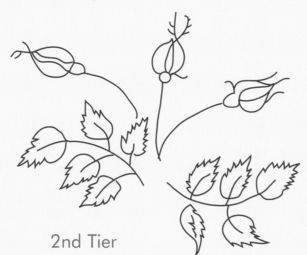

2nd Tier

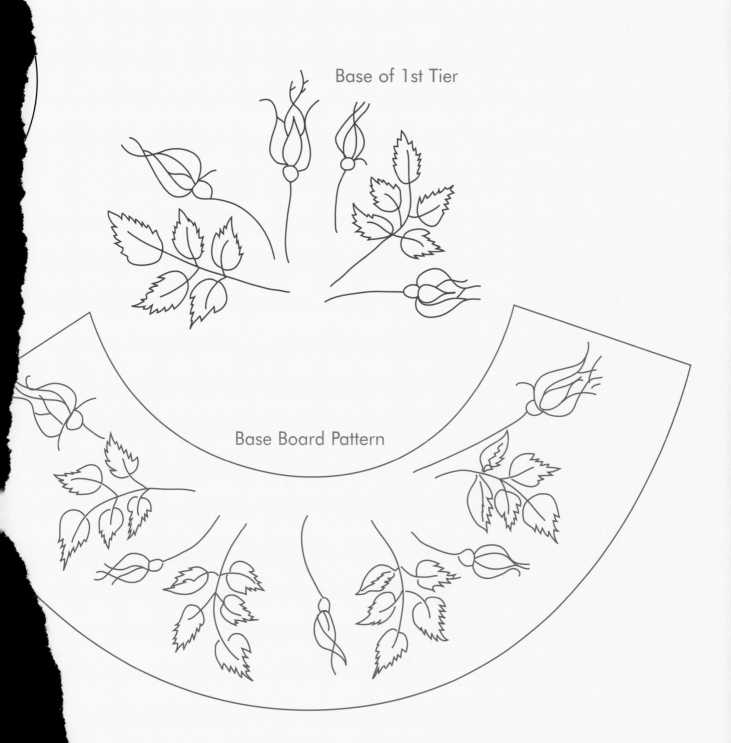

Base of 1st Tier

Base Board Pattern

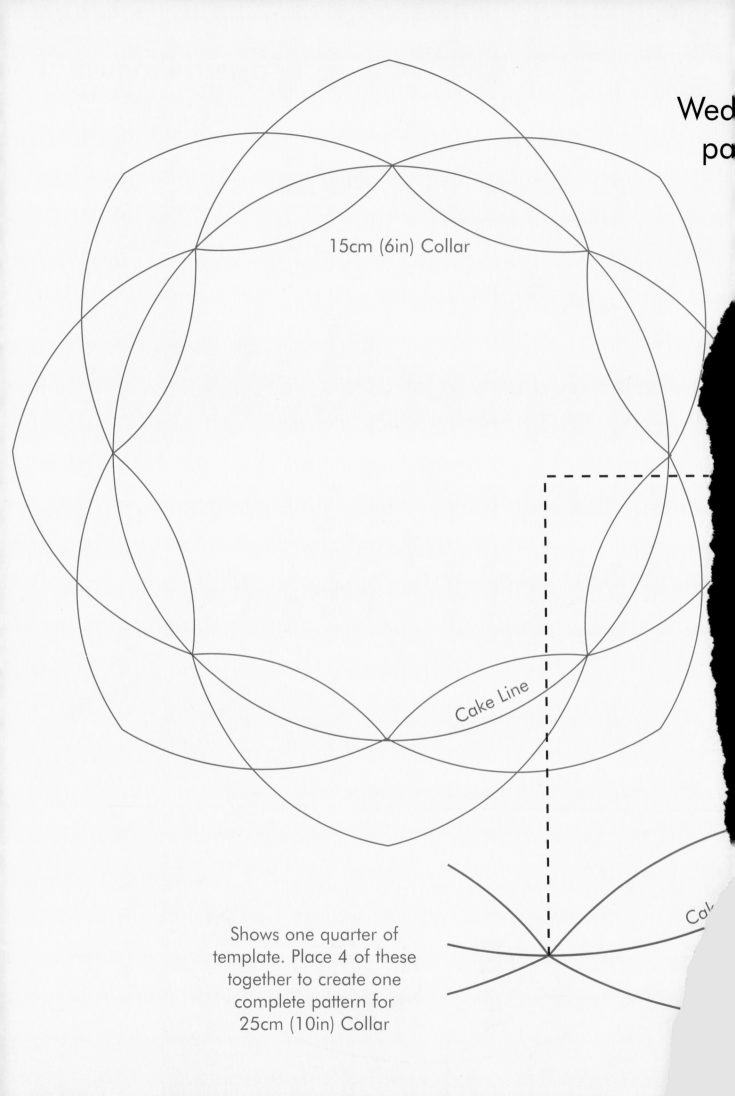

15cm (6in) Collar

Cake Line

Wed
pa

Col

Shows one quarter of
template. Place 4 of these
together to create one
complete pattern for
25cm (10in) Collar

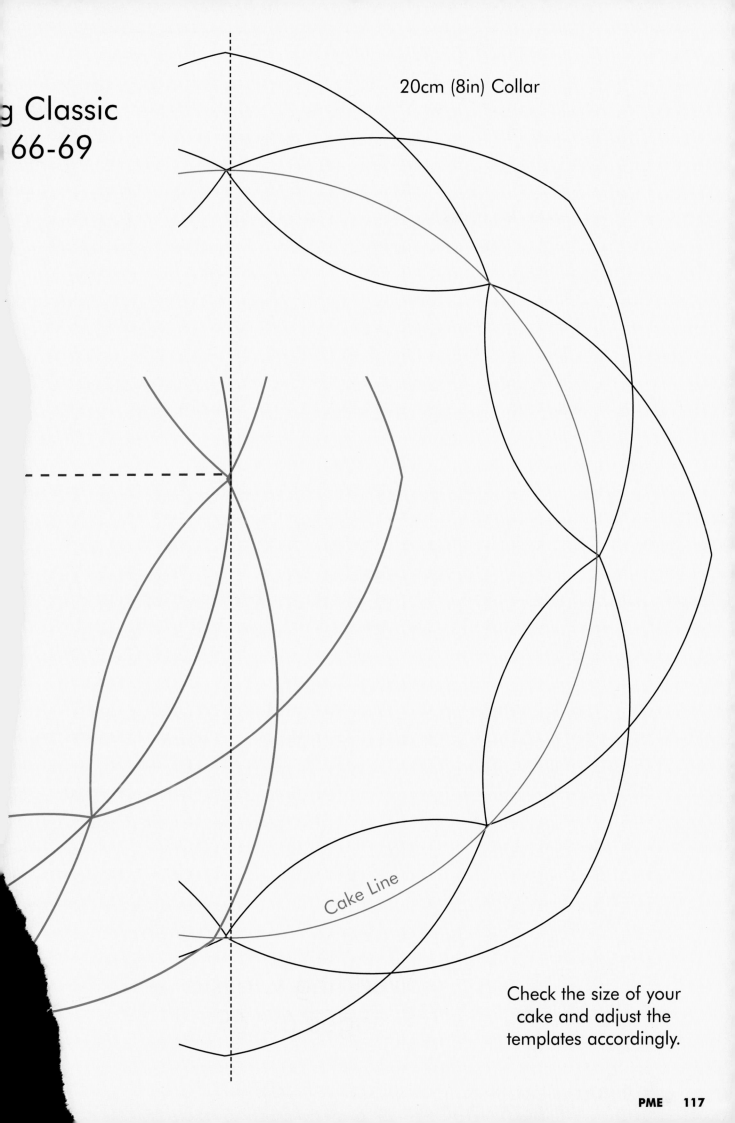

Classic
66-69

20cm (8in) Collar

Cake Line

Check the size of your
cake and adjust the
templates accordingly.

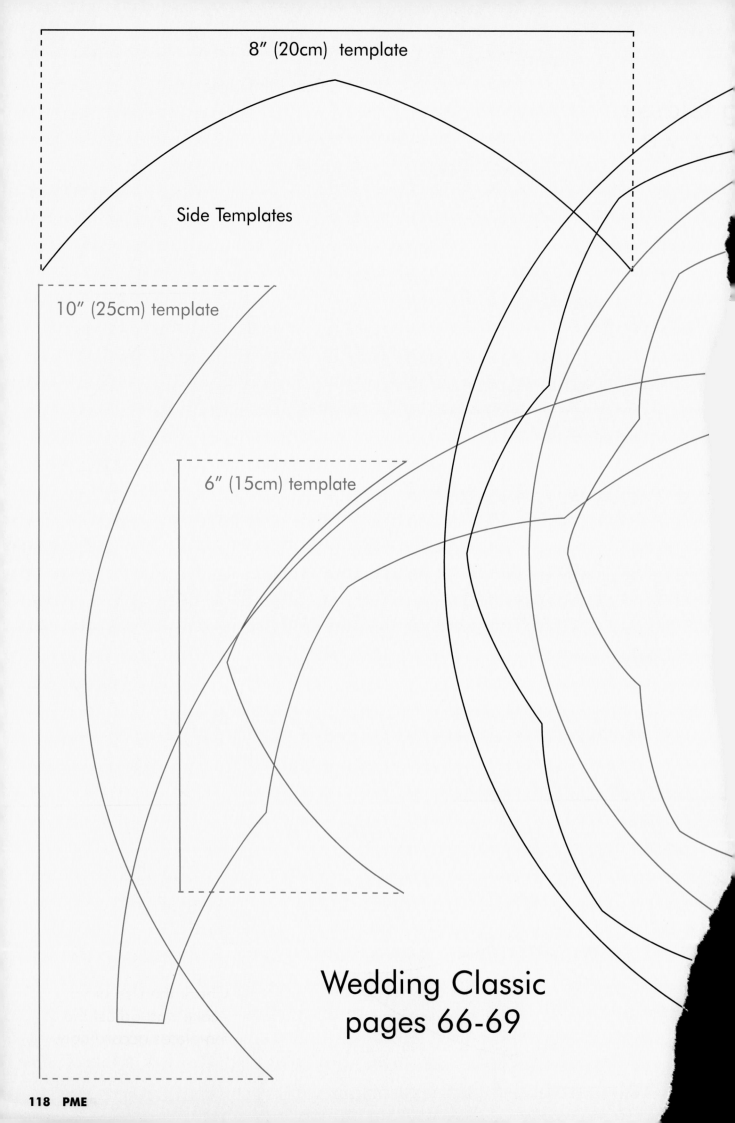

8" (20cm) template

Side Templates

10" (25cm) template

6" (15cm) template

Wedding Classic
pages 66-69

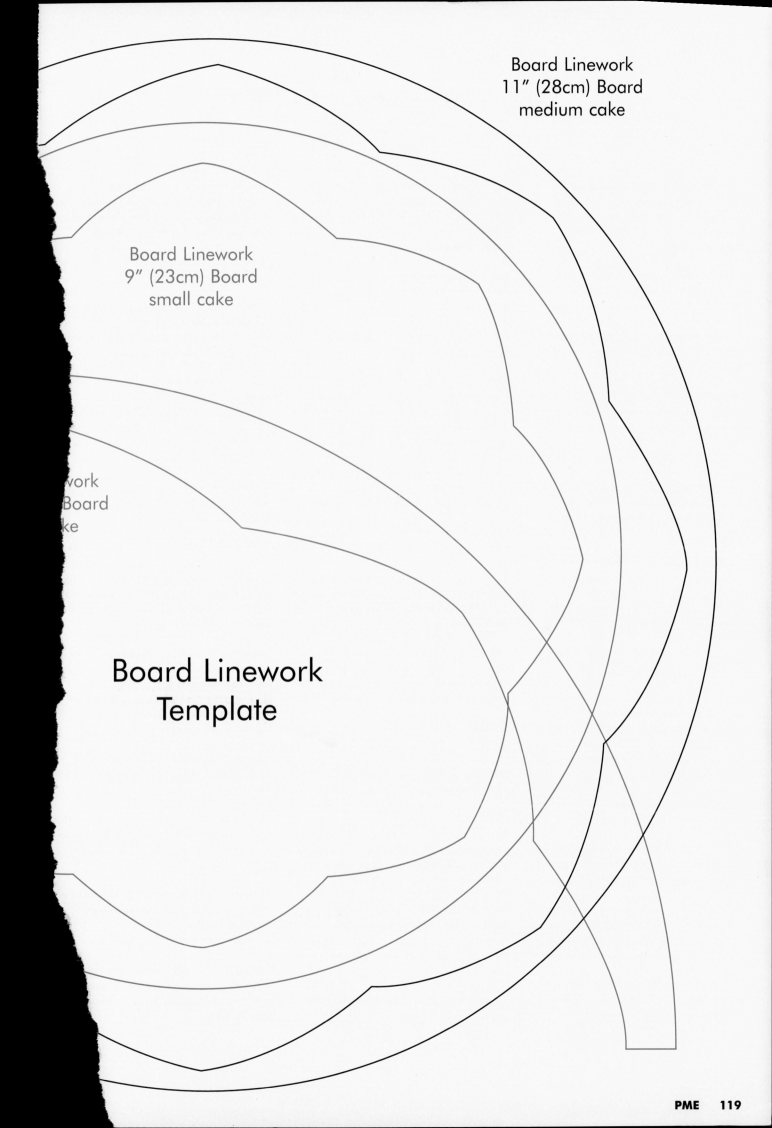

Board Linework
11" (28cm) Board
medium cake

Board Linework
9" (23cm) Board
small cake

...vork
...Board
...ke

Board Linework
Template

Glossary of Terms

Basket Weave - a traditional piping technique that requires a special piping tube. Basket weave indentations can also be created quickly using a basket weave textured rolling pin.

Blossom Plunger Cutters - used to make quick and simple flowers that can be used singly or in small groups.

Broderie Anglais - a fabric technique that resembles Embroderie Anglaise, sometimes known as eyelet work.

Dowelling Pegs - food grade plastic or wooden rods that are inserted into a cake to support additional cake tiers.

Calyx - a group of sepals/petals that protect the bud of a flower as it develops. Often seen as a green star shape at the base of the flower. Calyx cutters are also ideal for making a range of additional and fantasy flowers.

Collar - a royal icing border, often referred to as a runout or colour flow border.

Confectioners' Sugar - another name for icing sugar.

Copha - an alternative name for white vegetable fat or shortening.

Cornflour - sometimes known as cornstarch. Often used as a dusting powder for rolling out small pieces of paste as it is finer than icing sugar, but it should never be used when rolling out paste to cover a cake as this may encourage fermentation.

Crisco - a brand name for white vegetable fat.

Crimping - a decorative technique applied to freshly rolled out paste, using either open or closed adjustable crimpers .

Cutting Wheels - a modelling tool with small cutting wheels. Wonderful for cutting pastes to shape and ideal for creating small detailed cut out shapes.

Dresden tool - a name often given to a smooth backed modelling tool that is also known as a leaf shaper or veiner.

Edible Glue- sometimes also called sugar glue. A blend of edible gum e.g. Gum Tex, Tylose, CMC , Gum Tragacanth or Gum Arabic and water. Edible glue is used to join pieces of paste together.

Embossing- a design pressed into a paste, before it has set, using modelling tools, cutters or embossers.

Fondant Icing - another name for sugarpaste or roll out icing.

Garrett Frill - a technique that was created by Elaine Garrett from South Africa and is normally made using a Garrett Frill cutter used to cut out a sugarpaste shape. It is then frilled around the edges using a modelling tool.

Icing Ruler- a metal ruler with straight edges that is designed to give a smooth finish when coating the top of a cake with royal icing.

Icing Tips - an alternative name for icing tubes.

Inlay - a decorative technique where a cut out shaped piece of icing is removed from the cake covering and a textured or alternative coloured cut out piece inserted.

Leaf Cutters - available in different designs and sizes. Plunger leaf veining cutters also have the advantage of both cutting the leaf shape and adding embossed veining.

Nozzles - an alternative name for icing tubes.

Petal Dust - this is a powdered food colour that is also known as dusting powder or blossom tint.

Pillars - decorative supports used to separate tiered cakes. They are available in a variety of styles and designs and often used in conjunction with dowelling pegs.

Plaques - decorative cut out shapes of paste, that are often used to create interest to a cake design. Also ideal for inscriptions as they can be prepared prior to decorating the cake.

Powdered Sugar - another name for icing sugar.

Pressure Piping - a piping technique where varying degrees of pressure is applied to the piping bag as you work, this creates piped shapes of different sizes and outlines.

Quilting Tool - a small fine stitch wheel used to emboss stitching detail and effects.

Ribbed Rolling Pin - creates a ribbed design into freshly rolled out paste, ideal for texturing paste prior to cutting out shapes, sugar ribbons, fabric effects, and smocking.

Ribbon Insertion - a technique that gives impression ribbon has been threaded through the icing. A ribbon insertion blade used to create small cuts and then sugar ribbon is placed into the cuts, creating a threaded ribbon effect.

Scriber - a modelling tool used for transferring and tracing design guidelines onto a cake surface.

Smocking - a sugar embroidery technique, made using a ribbed rolling pin to create texture and tweezers to pinch out the design. Lines of coloured icing are then piped in a pattern to represent the thread and create the distinctive smocking style.

Smoother - a plastic cake decorating tool that will help to create a professional finish when coating cakes with sugarpaste or almond paste. Smooth over cakes coated with freshly rolled out paste to remove blemishes and marks.

Stamen - the central part of most flowers. Available in a wide variety of shapes, sizes and colours.

Tilting Turntable - this enables the cake to be set at an angle, creating a great advantage when working both on the cake sides and top.

Turntable - an extremely useful tool that for many cake decorators is essential item, available in a variety of heights, top diameters and also with a tilting top.

Veining Tools - used to create veining embossing detail on flowers and leaves known as a flower/leaf shaper and a Dresden tool.